For my mother, Doris Violet Howard, for her unconditional faith in me, love, and support. You're sadly missed. And to Dad, Sidney Stanley Howard, for helping instil a love of comedy and the natural world in us kids. I love you both.

My amazing Michelle. Such a wonderful, beautiful, kind, and inspirational force in my life. You're incredible and I love you so very much.

xx

THE DOCTOR WHO ART OF COLIN HOWARD

The right of Colin Howard to be identified as the Author of the Work has been asserted by him in accordance with the Copyright, Designs and Patents Act 1988.

Copyright © Colin Howard 2022
Artwork © Colin Howard 2022
Text © Candy Jar 2022

An Unofficial Doctor Who Book.

Published by
Candy Jar Books, Mackintosh House,
136 Newport Road, Cardiff, CF24 1DJ
www.candyjarbooks.co.uk

Book design by Shaun Russell, Colin Howard, and Philip Bates.
Editor: Philip Bates.
Editorial by Shaun Russell & Will Rees.
Doctor Who is © British Broadcasting Corporation 1963, 2022

All rights reserved.
No part of this publication may be reproduced, stored in a retrieval system, or transmitted at any time or by any means, electronic, mechanical, photocopying, recording or otherwise without the prior permission of the copyright holder. This book is sold subject to the condition that it shall not by way of trade or otherwise be circulated without the publisher's prior consent in any form of binding or cover other than that in which it is published.

(below) Danbury Mint, Day of the Daleks *plate.*

COLIN HOWARD BY MICHELLE HOWARD

Our house is full of treasures, drawers, boxes under the bed, cupboards, portfolios, shelves – all full of Colin's magnificent artwork, some recently rediscovered after clearing out an old outbuilding.

Each piece captures an era since we met nearly *thirty-five years ago*!

When I first met Colin, all long hair and cowboy boots and a cheeky twinkle in his eyes, he would sit on his bed for hours doing the most intricate black-and-white dot artwork. If you ever have an opportunity to look through this little portfolio, please do. It's a gem.

When I wasn't watching him work, he would show me his prize possessions: his treasured Chris Achilléos artbooks. His art hero and inspiration. I think the highlight of Colin's career was meeting Chris in 2019 and being blown away by his wonderful kindness, and generosity with his words and time. It's such a devastating loss that he has since passed; he will forever have a huge impact on Col.

I did manage to drag Colin away from his work at times. I love to travel, and he had little choice but to go where the flight I had booked took us. I hope his travels added to his art inspiration, especially when I decided, for my fortieth birthday, that we should go to South Africa and do volunteer work at a cheetah sanctuary in the middle of nowhere.

What an incredible experience that was – one that will stay with us forever. He left his artistic mark on the wall of the games room, with a stunning portrait of one of the cheetahs, created purely with a black marker pen straight onto a concrete wall.

When we returned, he painted a cheetah portrait onto canvas for me. It looks so real, you can almost run your fingers through the fur.

I don't think fans of sci-fi and art in general realise how much Colin has contributed over the last thirty-five years and that makes me sad. He has moved across so many different genres, it's quite astounding. He has far too much published work for one book.

I am so excited and proud of Colin. Proud, too, that this book has been created; seeing his amazing artwork in one place is a wonderful legacy.

CONTENTS

Colin Howard and Doctor Who	1	The King's Demons	58
Attack of the Cybermen	6	The Five Doctors	60
The Two Doctors	8	The Monster of Peladon	62
Planet of Evil	10	The Hand of Fear	64
The Green Death	12	The Leisure Hive	66
Inferno	14	The Awakening & Frontios	68
Ghost Light	16	The Happiness Patrol	70
Destiny of the Daleks	18	Revelation of the Daleks	72
The Seeds of Doom	20	Time-Flight	74
Kinda	22	Beast of Fang Rock	76
Snakedance	24	Doctor Who Magazine #167	78
The Android Invasion	26	Invasion of the Cat-People	80
Carnival of Monsters	28	Virgin Decalog	82
The Ribos Operation	30	The Masque of Mandragora Comic	84
The Pirate Planet	32	Doctor Who Magazine #192	86
The Stones of Blood	34	Doctor Who Classic Comics #11	88
The Androids of Tara	36	Classic Comics Autumn Holiday Special	90
The Power of Kroll	38	Doctor Who Classic Comics #18	92
The Armageddon Factor	40	Doctor Who Classic Comics #25	94
The Mark of the Rani	42	Doctor Who Classic Comics #27	96
Time and the Rani	44	The Eleven Doctors	98
Frontier in Space	46	Face the Raven	100
The Sea Devils	48	Scream of the Shalka	102
Warriors of the Deep	50	Animations	104
Paradise Towers	52	The Macra Terror	108
Survival	54	Timewave	110

TIMESLIDES: THE DOCTOR WHO ART OF COLIN HOWARD

FOREWORD BY COLIN BAKER

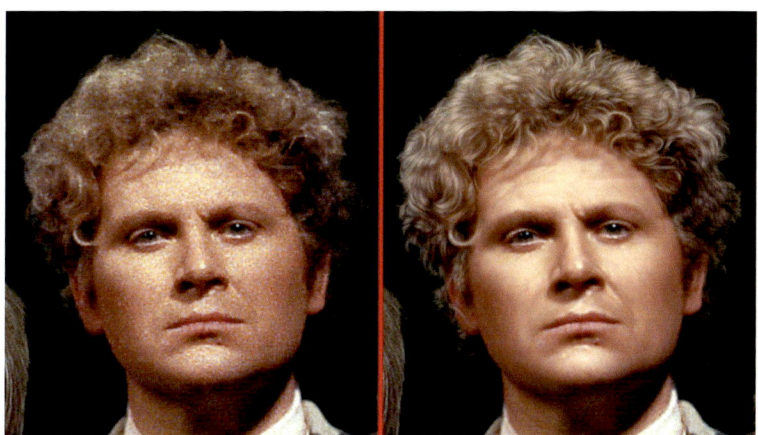

(left) An example of Colin Howard's digital enhancement work. On the left is a low-resolution photo; on the right is Colin's partially-painted upgrade.

Over the decades – four of them amazingly – since I became the Sixth Doctor in *Doctor Who*, I have been lucky enough to provide the inspiration for the work of many artists. I am, of course, aware that it is not due to any inherent irresistible qualities of my appearance that this creative outpouring has been provoked, but rather the wonderful programme with which I have become associated. This profusion of versions of 'Old Sixie' (as I refer to my alter ego) is amazing, even though the quality varies, from stick men with curls offered by young children – which are charming and I receive gratefully and take home to add to my collection – to workmanlike versions that, shall we say, don't necessarily make me feel I am looking in a mirror. Then there are the ones that are clearly me in every detail, and neither flatter nor distort, but are genuine works of art in their own right. The amount and variety of talented artists out there never fails to astonish me, and there are a handful that I know will always combine accuracy with imaginative flair and artistic creativity.

Colin Howard may well be the first of that handful whose next piece I await with eager anticipation. We first met in 1987 (when I was doing a play called *Corpse* at the Theatre Royal in Norwich) and then subsequently at a *Doctor Who* event in that city, when I saw some of his amazing black-and-white artwork representing Old Sixie, and of course, other Doctors. I expressed my admiration and we talked and became friends. Since then, I have followed his career and output with great interest, as he advanced steadily to become one of the best genre artists, as well as developing his talents in other directions. Before being asked to write this foreword, I was unaware of his superb animal portraits and regret not commissioning him before now to paint Henry, my anxious Jack Russell with an overbite.

Colin (great name by the way!) is kind enough to suggest that my encouragement and recommendation helped him progress, but his talent alone would have ensured that without any help from me.

His ability to continue his work is now being hampered increasingly by his recent diagnosis of Multiple Sclerosis, a difficult enough disease to live with for anyone, (a member of my own family has it), but so much worse for an artist like Colin, as his ability to create is being slowly eroded.

Thank you for your wonderful work, Colin, and the world of *Doctor Who* salutes you along with me – I know that for sure. The following pages exist as a tribute to your talent.

TIMESLIDES: THE DOCTOR WHO ART OF COLIN HOWARD

INTRODUCTION BY JOHN FREEMAN

Most of you reading this will know Colin Howard for his marvellous illustrations and paintings, particularly his *Doctor Who* work. It may surprise some of you, therefore, to learn that his first commissions for *Doctor Who Magazine,* back in the dim and distant past (well, the 1990s), were two one-page comic strips to accompany archives for, respectively, *The Masque of Mandragora* and *Terror of the Autons.*

The commissions came after I met Colin at a convention, like many new *DWM* contributors of the time, and after his first cover for Target Books, *Attack of the Cybermen*. I'm afraid neither of us can remember which convention, so it must have been good! He told me was keen to have a bash at drawing comic strips, and who was I to argue?

Both strips were a fun addition to the magazine, although I suspect comments from management on my budget-busting ways ensured only two were commissioned. But comic strips' loss was magazine covers' gain, Colin subsequently providing a number of those, his first, *Remembrance of the Daleks*, proving an excellent start.

Of course, this being a cover, some of the detail of his artwork, and of his subsequent work for *DWM*, was obscured by cover lines – a Dalek "claw" buried under the ubiquitous barcode on this issue. But now you have the chance to see the artworks as originally delivered to the Marvel UK offices, all those years ago.

Of course, Colin didn't just draw covers – he also provided several splendid illustrations, too, to accompany the magazine's text fiction: some suitably gothic art for a presentation of *Guardians of Prophecy*, an unmade Sixth Doctor story set on Traken, and written by Johnny Byrne, who you will know as the writer of not only *The Keeper of Traken* but *Warriors of the Deep*, and other TV stories.

It was always a pleasure working with Colin all those years ago. He was a frequent visitor to the Marvel offices even when he wasn't delivering work for the magazine, providing us with sneak peeks for his commissions for other *Who* publishers. Back then, artwork was still created physically, not just beamed to an editor via the Internet, and I have to say I miss the physical interaction such commissions afforded, not least because Colin was always at the office in time for lunch; getting together was much more fun than eating a sandwich at my desk! Colin always modest and often self-deprecating about the work, no matter how often I assured him of his obvious talents.

I'm so glad that, while it's been a long time since I commissioned a *Doctor Who Magazine* cover, Colin, and his partner Michelle have kept in touch down the years. And I'm truly honoured to have been asked to write this introduction for this collection. I do hope you enjoy it as much as I know I will, and, like me, it will remind us all just what a talented chap he is.

(left) Terror of the Autons *illustration (1990),*
published in the DWM *archive.*
(opposite, right) Me with a Mentor.
Pretty sure Kiv wants my head.

BIOGRAPHY

COLIN HOWARD AND DOCTOR WHO

I loved *Doctor Who* from a young age. Apparently my siblings – Sidney, Donna, and Tracey – and I liked to shout "Chumblies!", and pretended to be Daleks. It was written in the stars!

I was born on 25th November 1965 to Sidney and Doris Howard, in the market town of Harleston, Norfolk, in the Waveney Valley, just on the border with Suffolk. Back then, we had three channels and not a lot on! I always loved fantasy movies like those by Ray Harryhausen, and was eager to watch anything similar, so I suppose that's how I first got into *Doctor Who*.

My father was the son of former farm managers, Reginald and Lillian, who lived in Harleston's oldest property, a coaching inn (essentially a rest-stop for weary travellers) at Old Market Place. Dad served as a radio operator in Korea for his national service, and, when he returned, became an apprentice for a local firm where he learned to be a builder. He actually did work for Tristram Cary (who provided incidental music for numerous serials like *Marco Polo, The Gunfighters*, and *The Mutants*), who lived in nearby Diss, so I think he was working on *The Daleks' Master Plan* or something at the time.

We lived in a sprawling multi-levelled house that's recently been renovated. I have memories of sitting halfway up a narrow staircase, just close enough to the sitting room door to enable me to peer through a gap and watch black-and-white TV shows late into the evening. Often I'd nod off and take a tumble downstairs, and give the whole game away…

It was in that house that I first remember watching *Doctor Who*. My oldest clear memory is *Spearhead from Space*, Jon Pertwee's first story. Yes, there was a nearby tailors with mannequins that terrified me ever afterwards – they, too, might smash out of their glass encasements to spread the Nestene Consciousness throughout my hometown!

In the late 1960s, Dad decided he wanted a change and took a job at Richard Clay Publishers. Around this time, Dad also bought a plot of land from his own father and built a bungalow on Straight Lane. We moved there in 1970. But while working on a book binding machine press, his right hand was crushed in a press. The injury was horrible and resulted in reconstructive surgery, which involved some of

his knuckles having to be reversed. I remember us being ferried up to Norwich by a family friend to visit Dad in hospital while he recovered.

Never one to just sit back and moan, Dad taught himself to use his hand again (and was even able to re-learn his snooker cue action, a sport he was very proficient at). He then became self-employed as a builder, painter and decorator. I'd often go and help him on site and pick up skills. There, a love of design seemed to rub off on me.

I had always drawn from a young age. I loved birds, and animals in general, as well as space and science fiction. I was an avid ornithologist and as a family we'd often go on birdwatching trips: very handy as Harleston is in the middle of the countryside, so there was a great abundance and variation of wildlife.

We'd watch *Doctor Who* as a family, we all had a copy of *The Doctor Who Monster Book* (1975), and in school my sisters and I would re-enact scenes like the Cybermen versus Vogans from *Revenge of the Cybermen*. I took things to another level though. I collected the stand-up cards Weetabix issued in the '70s. It was these that inspired my first *Doctor Who* artwork, when I drew a Weetabix Ogron on the wall of my bedroom, which was then covered up by awful woodchip; it should still be there in Straight Lane, lurking beneath the wallpaper like the warning to Sally Sparrow in *Blink*!

TIMESLIDES: THE DOCTOR WHO ART OF COLIN HOWARD

I especially loved the Target work of Chris Achilléos. Every time we went for a day trip, if we passed a WH Smith, I would plead with my parents to get the new paperback. I was more smitten by the show than the rest of my siblings, and I became an avid collector of the novels and anything else linked to the show, continuing to watch even when the rest of my family's interest had waned.

Doctor Who Magazine (*DWM*) was a favourite. I redrew the early comic strips into my own home-produced specials, presenting them alongside crosswords like those from the early *Doctor Who Weekly* issues.

Villains and monsters always particularly interested me. I was more Green Goblin than Spider-Man, more Joker than Batman.

Joining the local *Doctor Who Appreciation Society* group led me to fanzine work, illustrating for *Cloister Bell* and *Cosmic Masque* in the '80s, further fuelling my burgeoning ambition to become a *Doctor Who* cover artist like my hero, Christos. I'd now seriously set my sights on that goal.

I carried on flooding *Doctor Who Magazine* with submissions, and my persistence paid off when John Freeman became editor. He commissioned me to do a full-page comic strip for *The Masque of Mandragora* archive feature, then another for *Terror of the Autons*, a similar article. That was my in-road with *Doctor Who* artwork. At the time, I was already doing some art for the *White Dwarf* magazine from Games Workshop, but sadly, they never returned any art – *DWM* was better in that regard!

Artists have these wonderfully lit large rooms, a couple of easels laden with paints, tonnes of brushes, and a nice chair for models to drape themselves over, posing for their turn on canvas. Right?

My workspaces have always been a tad different to that. When I started out doing illustrations, I could be found bent double on the side of my bunkbed, with a sketchpad on my lap, dotting away with a Rotring pen. But now I was a verified pro, I resurrected something I'd made at secondary school: a desk that would fold away. Because of my father's job, I was interested in carpentry at a young age, and hey, we were a family of six, living in a bungalow, and we needed the space. It would sit flat against my wall when not in use. Then Dad made me an angled A-frame out of wood, so for my paintings, notably *Attack of the Cybermen* and my *DWM* covers, I had this A-frame bolted onto my folding desk. I'd sit in the front room in Harleston, working away, often with the TV in the corner and the bustle of family life going on around me.

After lunch, Mum would often sit watching daytime soaps in that front room, so we spent a lot of time together. Plus, we shared a great love of classic adventure and horror films and would go to the cinema to see the latest *Sinbad* movie and suchlike as a family. Mum was always incredibly supportive and encouraging of my art. She must have recognised the extent of my passion; she was always a deeply empathetic woman. When we were all a bit older, she got a job as a home-help for the elderly, and would cycle across town, doing housework and shopping for them.

My dad has a terrific sense of humour. Together we would watch shows like *Monty Python's Flying Circus* (1969-74) and *The Two Ronnies* (1971- 87), through to Spike Milligan's *Q* series (1969-82). This instilled a love of comedy in me, something that's proved essential in life, helping me deal with adversity in all its forms.

In later years, Mum battled breast cancer, courageously and with good humour, and with the help of chemotherapy she received the all-clear. Nobly, she returned to her home-help job and continued for a few years before the cancer returned. I knew things were getting bad when she would come into the lounge and just drift off to sleep on the sofa. She eventually lost her battle with it in hospital on 3rd February 1991. She never got to see my VHS work, but she did get to meet

BIOGRAPHY

(opposite) "There's only my will because I possess the Key to Time…!" The full VHS sleeves for season sixteen.
(left) My painting of Jabari, a gift for Michelle.
(below) My beloved Norwich fan group. I'm middle row, third from right, looking chilled with my legs crossed.

Michelle a few times, and that's more important – that the two amazing women in my life got on.

Michelle and I met at The Bell Hotel in Norwich a week before the Great Storm of 1987. I couldn't believe this beautiful, intelligent, caring, and funny girl might be interested in me, but it seemed my luck was in. We started seeing each other regularly at weekends: I'd travel up to Norwich and crash at friends' houses; then, after five years of dating, we got married, on 18th August 1992, at The Octagon Chapel in Norwich. We moved into a house on Cozens Road, part of the housing estate built by the Colman's Mustard company for its workers.

My studio there was a small entry room in a two-bedroom terraced house. And I'd sit there with that same desk and the same A-frame. That's where I painted the VHS covers. Now, I've got equipment littered all over: I retired the desk I made, but I've still got Dad's A-frame, which is now attached to a shop-bought desk with an adjacent PC and tablet, overlooking our back garden in the upstairs bedroom. There are distractions out the window – if you're lucky. I'll see an occasional buzzard, or a squirrel slipping around in winter. I've got a desk in the front room too, where I've got a new Wacom tablet, on which I worked on the The Evil of the Daleks animation. It's a difficult discipline working on a graphics tablet, especially from a sketch on a different screen. That's how I did the other animations.

In the mid-'90s, Shaun, a good friend of mine, lent me a small CRT monitor and an old Compaq desktop PC, on which was installed some newfangled creation called an "art program". I dabbled with this new invention and learned to modify my painting techniques. I had always been interested in technology, having graduated to a PlayStation from the Grandstand and Atari consoles of my youth. But I had been a year too old to study Computer Science at secondary school, so this was a whole new world of imagery for me.

I ended up supplying some backgrounds for a *Hercules* movie tie-in for the PlayStation, with its heavily stylised trees, as well as covers for Sega's *Mean Machines* magazine (1990-92). However, these were painted traditionally, then sent away as I always had done.

My approach to digital art has never been separate

TIMESLIDES: THE DOCTOR WHO ART OF COLIN HOWARD

to my analogue work, i.e. make a traditional sketch then scan it in to work on further. More recently, I'd sketch straight onto my tablet, going in layers from the background and proceeding forwards. Working on the old graphics tablets was like rubbing your stomach and patting your head at the same time. You're looking over at what you're creating remotely on the monitor, while moving your pen in your usual drawing position elsewhere. It takes some getting used to, but, like most things, gets easier with practise, and I am now comfortable with both.

I can still produce art but, owing to my multiple sclerosis (MS), only at a much slower rate than I did before. I have to be careful not to drop valuable equipment, due to the reduced feeling and numbness in my hands, as well as infrequent spasms.

I don't think people generally know too much about MS. It doesn't get much media coverage and symptoms are very different for everyone affected.

I first started to become aware something wasn't right around 2008; it always felt like my shoes were too tight, then like a small ball of lint was in my shoe under my toes, with accompanying tingling which eventually spread up both legs. Despite many trips to my then-GP, who espoused a trapped nerve theory, Michelle insisted I see a specialist sports therapist, who, after examining me, suggested I was referred to a neurologist for an MRI scan to investigate further.

In 2010, I was diagnosed with progressive MS, the scan revealing damage/lesions in my brain and the central nervous system in my neck too. Multiple sclerosis causes some of the body's B cells (the trained heroes of the COVID-19 vaccine) to effectively go rogue and attack the myelin covering your nerves. Think of it as picking the rubberised protective flex from electrical wiring and the damage that creates. The body can re-route via other nerves, but soon those options run out.

The most common form of MS is relapsing-remitting, where you suffer 'incidents' that you can slowly recover from. My form, primary progressive, is a gradual worsening of symptoms from which you don't recover. I initially wanted to call this book *Icebergs* in relation to the Fifth Doctor's speech in *The Five Doctors* as the Timescoop captures his other selves: 'great chunks of my past floating away like melting icebergs...' It nicely summed up how I felt watching MS slowly erode my abilities.

I'd mostly managed to conceal my symptoms for

Mum and Dad on their wedding day (28th March 1959).

years, but gradually, issues with balance and walking made that impossible. In recent years, it's started affecting my hands and arms the way it did initially with my legs. I'm currently on a six-monthly drug infusion treatment of Ocrevus at the hospital, which is supposed to halt symptom progression. The pandemic unfortunately affected the continuity of this treatment while I was working on *The Evil of the Daleks* animation.

I still try to be a part of the wider *Doctor Who* community as much as I can. I got to see Colin Baker recently at a *Doctor Who Appreciation Society* Capitol event, for instance. I sat opposite him, biding my time because I have met him before, through the local *Doctor Who* group. We all went to see him in *Corpse* (1987), a play at the Norwich Theatre Royal. We'd had a memorabilia sale for charity and there we presented Colin with a cheque for the Foundation for the Study of Infant Deaths (for which he became a trustee and then, from 1997 to 2005, chairman). He was an absolutely lovely guy. I showed him some of my work, and he was quite impressed, which meant everything. Later, he came to one of the conventions we'd organised, and as a result of that, he wrote a reference

BIOGRAPHY

that got me taken a bit more seriously at the BBC, Target owners WH Allen, and places like that. It was pretty damn good to have a reference from the Doctor himself!

I've changed quite a lot from how I looked back in the '80s; I used to have really long back-combed dark hair, and always wore cowboy boots, skinny jeans, band t-shirts – I was a bit of a metal head, really. Now, I've got short grey hair and a beard. So, all those decades later, in the Capitol, having sat patiently while he talked to Katy Manning, introducing myself with a thank you for his letter all those years ago, it was wonderful to see the penny drop, and the dawn of realisation come over his face.

And he remembered me, so that was fantastic.

(top right) Colin with Red Dwarf *artwork.*
(bottom, left) Cover art for Who on Earth is Tom Baker?
(bottom, right) Logopolis *artwork.*

TIMESLIDES: THE DOCTOR WHO ART OF COLIN HOWARD

ATTACK OF THE CYBERMEN (TARGET)

Written by Eric Saward. Starring the Sixth Doctor and Peri Brown. Published on 20th April 1989.
"The TARDIS, when working properly is capable of many amazing things. Not unlike myself."

My only Target cover came about through submitting work for inclusion in the Peter Haining books, *The Key to Time* and *25 Glorious Years* – probably more so the latter because I sent in a lot of A4-heavy pixelation portraitures. Mike Brett, the art editor of W.H. Allen at the time, saw them and asked me if I painted as well. It was my big chance to achieve my childhood dream of doing a *Doctor Who* novel cover, so I said, 'Yeah, I can paint!' It wasn't fundamentally untrue: I could and had, but more infrequently since school.

I've still got Mike's letter, dated 19th August 1988; since I'd left school in 1982, I'd mostly focused on more cost-effective black-and-white illustrations, using a Rotring pen, for Games Workshop's *White Dwarf* magazine.

At the time, it was probably the most anxious I'd ever been in my life. My abiding memory of the painting process was my hand shaking because I was so nervous! I wanted to do as well as I possibly could, and once I was as satisfied as I ever would be, I sent a couple of designs in for *Attack of the Cybermen*. Mike went with the one without Colin Baker. The other design had the Cyber base and a large picture of the Sixth Doctor, more the traditional look, but at the time they were moving away from having the Doctor's likeness on the covers.

The actual painting was only about A4, on cartridge paper, not on card or board. And although it looks fairly good reduced down, it's still pretty crude, certainly compared to the standard that I was able to achieve later on. I think that was the main reason I didn't get asked to do any more, which was a great shame because I was so pleased about the opportunity.

At the time, my mother was just in the process of battling breast cancer. She got to see my one Target cover in 1989, but she never got to see my VHS covers, as she passed away in 1991, shortly before I married Michelle. She'd always championed my being an artist and wanted me to follow my heart, so it was awful that she wasn't there a few years later when I finally achieved success with the VHS range; she only saw my one Target cover, followed by more years of rejections.

But in the end I refined my painting technique, and eventually John Freeman allowed me to do covers for *Doctor Who Magazine*. And from then on, my work just improved steadily over time.

Still, it was absolutely fantastic to hold in my hands something that I'd always wanted to do. As a kid, I had always been fired up by these Target novels, which kept me entertained on trips to the coast or up to Norwich with my family. It was awesome to join that pantheon of artists.

ATTACK OF THE CYBERMEN

(above) Target book cover for Attack of the Cybermen.
(opposite) 1990 illustration.

TIMESLIDES: THE DOCTOR WHO ART OF COLIN HOWARD

THE TWO DOCTORS (VHS)

Starring the Second and Sixth Doctors. Released in November 1993.
"When you travel around as much as I do, it's almost inevitable that you'll run into yourself at some point."

I had an interview at the BBC to see if they thought I was worthy of doing the VHS covers. Sarah Andrews, the editor of the VHS range, offered me a choice between either *The Two Doctors* or, I think, *Resurrection of the Daleks* [which would be released on VHS at the same time as *The Two Doctors*].

I love the monsters of *Doctor Who* and this was a chance to do the Sontarans alongside Patrick Troughton *and* Colin Baker – that wasn't a hard decision for me to make! I was a fairly young child when *The Time Warrior* aired, and as I was a stocky little thing, I really identified with the Sontarans. And, of course, I could do the three-digit Sontaran hands by putting my middle and forefinger together, and my little finger and ring finger together, and do that with both hands.

First I sent in my pencil sketches for the cover, with Jacqueline Pearce as Chessene, flanked by a couple of Sontarans.

My only recurring issue with the finished covers was that they would always crop the artwork. I'd make really careful measurements and upscale to find the correct sizes, in order to do a larger A3 or A2 painting. You had to look at how previous covers were all laid out and take into account how far the titles came down, precisely where the "Starring COLIN BAKER and PATRICK TROUGHTON" caption would be, and where the PG ratings and BBC logo would go. But then, no matter how much bleed you gave the artwork, to enable the designers to retain central areas, you'd see the cover proof and think, "Oh great, they've chopped a bit more off!"

I'd feel somewhat deflated when the cover proofs arrived, but the thing is, this was my dream job, something I'd wanted as a small child. And I'd now achieved my goal in life. There couldn't be anything better, surely, than doing these covers. So I just had to go, "Okay, that's not how I envisaged it, but that's how it's come out," and accept that. All the covers do essentially work, just to varying degrees. It was a roulette wheel.

Traditionally, you'd send artwork in on an illustration board. But rather than flat scan it or photograph it, the BBC would drum-scan the artwork; this was a large cylinder that would rotate over the reader to pick up the image. There was a lot of scope for catastrophe and for the art to be damaged! That's one of the reasons I started to just work on the equivalent of a light card, which had a bit of flexibility.

Also, back then, you were at the mercy of the Post Office or whichever delivery company had hold of your art. There was always a bit of a worry that there would be damage, which I believe did happen to a couple – and one was even stolen (which I'll come back to).

(above) Original sketch for The Two Doctors *VHS.*
(opposite) Original VHS artwork.

THE TWO DOCTORS (VHS)

TIMESLIDES: THE DOCTOR WHO ART OF COLIN HOWARD

PLANET OF EVIL (VHS)

Starring the Fourth Doctor and Sarah Jane Smith. Released in December 1993.
"Here on Zeta Minor is the boundary between existence as you know it and the other universe which you just don't understand!"

With *The Two Doctors*, I was following a style format that was used quite heavily back then: essentially, a fairly flat background with a geometric influence to the layout. When I handed it in, one of the first things Sarah Andrews said was, "We want to break away from that. Make it more sci-fi and action-packed."

That's why there was a big change of style for the *Planet of Evil* cover, a story that I think was repeated once, maybe twice when I was young, in the heady days we would actually get a *Doctor Who* repeat on the BBC. It had made quite an impression on me.

I knew certain things *had* to make the cover: the wonderful Lis Sladen, and the Jekyll and Hyde transformation of Professor Sorensen. And of course, it was my first official go at that scarf.

I also managed to weave in some of that fantastical jungle planet set, which had always reminded me of those classic (and sometimes not so classic) B-movies of my childhood, like, most notably, *Forbidden Planet* (1956).

I loved the human explorers and rescue team being at the mercy of this strange, barely visible Anti-Matter Beast, which could kill and dehydrate a body as it brushed and rustled past. But something I wasn't able to work in was the Doctor's toffee tin, in which he stored the crystals from Zeta Minor. Perhaps inspired by this, through a relative I'd managed to obtain a tobacco tin, and in that, I stored my prized *Doctor Who* Weetabix stand-up figure cards – *Who* treasure for a young fan.

There's another version of *Planet of Evil*, as I also produced a portfolio version, which helped get me the job. This original artwork was A2 in an attempt to avoid photographic reduction and cropping.

(left) The portfolio version of Planet of Evil *(1992).*
(above) The original sketch for Planet of Evil VHS.
(Opposite) Original VHS artwork.

PLANET OF EVIL (VHS)

TIMESLIDES: THE DOCTOR WHO ART OF COLIN HOWARD

THE GREEN DEATH (VHS)

Starring the Third Doctor and Jo Grant. Released in October 1996.
"Wealth in our time!"

The *Green Death* was actually done in 1993 too. It was the last one from the first batch that I was commissioned for. By 1996 I was wondering if it'd ever see the light of day, because at that stage, I'd been told that I was now surplus to requirements and had been replaced.

[*The Green Death* was scheduled for March 1994, but was initially delayed due to BBC Two repeating the serial at the start of that year. It was then pencilled in for April 1996, before BBC Video reportedly pushed back multiple releases until after the release of *The TV Movie*, starring Paul McGann. Jon Pertwee's passing in May 1996 saw it make its way back into that year's schedule.]

I found a black-and-white Pertwee reference photo from *DWM* (which I had to colourise) and a nice one of Katy Manning when she's imprisoned by the Master in *Frontier in Space*. I then had to come up with an unusual layout utilising the giant maggots with their snapping little jaws.

I think the lack of available reference material back then was both good and bad: good because it meant *DWM* constantly required illustrations to avoid reprinting the same publicity stills all the time, which led to me working for John Freeman; and bad because it made my job harder!

We have the Internet now. We have tonnes of resources for *Doctor Who*. Back then, however, you had to collect magazines and books, and find reference material wherever you could. The Peter Haining books were good, but were done in the 1980s. So I'd have to watch the wobbly VHS copies that would do the rounds before the official VHSes came out. Being a member of the local *Doctor Who Appreciation Society*, I'd get illicit pirate copies from Australia, taken from ABC I think, and other places, then end up home-copying them, to amass a library of existing *Who*. Anywhere that commissioned me was basically assuming that, like most fans, I would have my own archive of stuff that I could look at.

I'd collected *DWM* since the first issue, and because I was involved in fanzines, I'd produced a glossary of images for future reference. It was a case of noting down which issues had decent photographs; whether they were in colour or black-and-white (for fanzine work the latter would be fine, but paintings for *DWM* or VHSes would require cross-referencing to find the right colour swatches); what expressions the Doctors, companions, or

antagonists had; and what page they were on. I could check this hand-typed resource to find out where to look for a specific photo.

All of my VHS work was done on what is essentially a thick card – like an illustration or mounting board, but thinner and more flexible. Canvases are nice, but if you're working at a small scale, those dimples show up. I didn't want those on the VHS covers. This type of card was my go-to, particularly when I knew the BBC used a drum-scanner, which could strip the picture from the backing or leave a massive tear. This was a more flexible board that could be wrapped onto a drum without needing to be pried away from surroundings, and could also be photographed to get a good quality image.

*(above) The original sketch for
The Green Death VHS.
(opposite) Original VHS artwork.*

THE GREEN DEATH (VHS)

TIMESLIDES: THE DOCTOR WHO ART OF COLIN HOWARD

INFERNO (VHS)

Starring the Third Doctor, Liz Shaw, and the Brigadier. Released in May 1994.
"If you break through the Earth's crust now, you'll release forces you never dreamed existed!"

I was normally given a deadline of about two weeks, which was a bit ridiculous, especially when you had to research everything yourself, get a sketch approved, and then deliver the final artwork. It was always a mad dash to make the deadline. I would ask them, "Please can you just let me know the schedule so that I can pre-plan and work out conceptually what I'd like to do for each one?"

But even then, you'd be at the mercy of a schedule change at the eleventh hour, which is what happened with *Inferno*. I was busy painting *Revelation of the Daleks*, which was the next release in the schedule, when without warning the release was dropped, and I was asked to do *Inferno* instead.

The only problem was my wife and I had our honeymoon booked. When we'd got married in 1992, we hadn't had one. As a result of those Hoover flights, we'd finally got our honeymoon out of them – a free return trip to the States, and we went to see our friend, Bev, in New York.

[In late 1992, the British division of The Hoover Company ran a promotion that offered two round-trip plane tickets to the United States to anyone purchasing £100 or more of Hoover products. This was an effort to drive up sales during the early 1990s' recession, but the company underestimated demand and tried to renege on the offer – unsuccessfully.]

We had freezing cold weather in New York: 8 to 12ft walls of ice had piled up and reduced all the freeways to maybe two lanes, and there was a lot of skidding. It was fun.

Nonetheless, you never wanted to let the BBC down. You're their regular guy, so if you don't deliver, they still need that artwork from somewhere. If you want a good working relationship with the BBC, you help out as best you can. This was my dream job, something I'd wanted to do since I was a kid. I didn't want to be stuck on the sidelines again; I'd experienced years of that on book work.

So I painted *Inferno* in three days!

I think I had half a day to do the pencils, and luckily, they approved that straight away. Then I had three days in which to paint it and get it dispatched to the BBC, then get on our flight. You try to keep good working hours in the day, but often, you'd start a bit earlier, finish a little later; if it's a really tight brief, you work into the evenings and then into the night.

A lot of heavy hours went into *Inferno*, which is why it only features three main elements: the alternative Brigadier with his eye patch, the Primord, and Jon Pertwee in the foreground, plus the erupting refinery, the oncoming doom bought about by Stahlman's drilling.

It's quite a bold cover, thanks to the strong colours, reflecting volcanic activity and the destruction of Earth (albeit in another dimension).

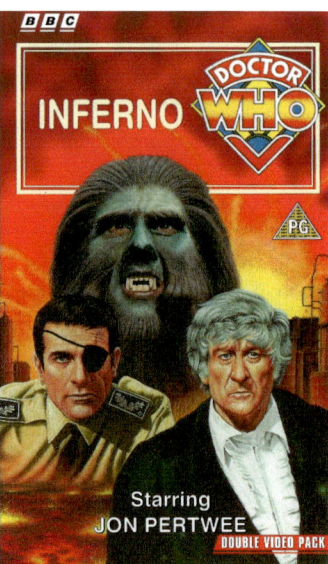

When choosing a palette, the obvious thing to ask is, "Is the story space related? And if so, how can I work that element into it?" It was far more difficult on some of the historical stories, like *The Mark of the Rani*, for instance, and *The Green Death*, set down in coal mines, etc. But I still managed to pop a nebula cloud on the background of *The Green Death*, just because it's something I enjoy doing when airbrushing – plus, there's that sequence on Metebelis III.

(above) The VHS sleeve for Inferno.
(opposite) Original VHS artwork.

INFERNO (VHS)

TIMESLIDES: THE DOCTOR WHO ART OF COLIN HOWARD

GHOST LIGHT (VHS)

Starring the Seventh Doctor and Ace. Released in May 1994.
"All organic life will be destroyed in the firestorm and when this world is destroyed there will be no more change, no more evolution and no more life..."

Here's the classic Victorian haunted house, with these nightmarish Husk creatures. So we've got the cold, harsh sky, the lightning forks guiding your eyes, running down either side of a Husk's face, to add that spooky element to the piece; and then contrasting with that, down at the bottom, we've got the warmth of the spacecraft console. I positioned the glowing dais around Sophie's heart – Ace is the heart of *Ghost Light*.

I added in a nice moody Sylvester McCoy reference image that was used a lot at the time, bleeding in with the illuminated text that kept coming up throughout the serial. This is one of my favourites.

I'm certainly not averse to the odd haunted house story. I always loved shows like *Sapphire & Steel*, and on a Friday night growing up, I could generally be found watching horror films with my mum on BBC Two. My brother and father would be in the front room watching the football, and we'd be in the kitchen, watching an old Hammer Horror or another classic black-and-white film on a little portable TV, while on the production line and sorting football snacks and cheese on toast for them.

I know a lot of artists trace their designs and reproduce them on a separate piece so they can keep their originals. But I was just a self-taught bod starting out, so I always painted directly over my pencils and used that as a guide for the final work. It was so much easier that way. It's a great shame that for the majority of these VHSes, I lost the original pencils. I'd make photocopies to remind myself what I intended to do, then take my original sketch on card, mask off around it to create a border, airbrush the area to create a background, and then work that up, layer on layer, popping in all the effects. Then I'd go more middle ground and work towards the foreground and blend everything together.

You're just layering over a layer over a layer, working towards your main viewpoint. That way, it's easier not to go over things that you spent time painting meticulously; otherwise, you risk an accident, mistakenly airbrushing over a section without masking it off first. It's a logical progression. It was the same technique that they used in the Disney animations. You have a background and then you have multiple transparent cell layers in front of that, and each one of those has a background element – for instance, more trees for characters to pass between, and then more bushes in the foreground, up to a house or a barrel or something like that. That gives you the freedom to alter and reposition things, rather than being cemented to your original decision. You really get a sense of depth. Plus, you're not wasting too much time painting something you don't need to – you always have a very fast turnaround on these covers.

That was the same process, essentially, that I used to create the paintings.

(left) The published cover for Ghost Light. *Notice how it was cropped so much, one of the husks is cut in half.*
(opposite) Original VHS artwork.

GHOST LIGHT (VHS)

TIMESLIDES: THE DOCTOR WHO ART OF COLIN HOWARD

DESTINY OF THE DALEKS (VHS)

Starring the Fourth Doctor, the Second Romana and K9. Released in July 1994.
"The Dalek fleet will be wiped from the heavens and nothing will stand in the way of our conquest of the galaxy..."

This is my only ...*of the Daleks* VHS cover, unbelievably. By the time I came into the VHS range, a lot of the stories with classic monsters had already been done. I got a few, but not loads. I would've liked to have done any of the early Tom Baker stories, and obviously some more Jon Pertwee ones too. Or really, anything with what I felt to be an iconic monster. I would have loved to do *Doctor Who and the Silurians*, but I missed the boat on that one. And I absolutely adored the Cybermen, but they were often assigned elsewhere. At least I managed to sneak in the Cybermen for *The Five Doctors*, somewhat under the radar!

The Movellans were an interesting concept, beautiful on the exterior but essentially humanoid Daleks with a thirst for conquest. That gave me the excuse to pop the lovely Suzanne Danielle, who played the Movellan soldier, Agella, on the cover, to represent the cold but stunning aliens.

The Movellan ship was such a nice model shot too. Like most young lads, I liked my spaceships! That was a cool design, with the contra-rotating lower section that buried itself down to the entrance and exit hatch. It enabled me to mix it up a bit, to meld background elements together to create the sandy area that the Dalek was sitting on, and then blend that away to the spacecraft.

Getting location and model shots for reference was especially hard. Most were either black-and-white or standard photo references that weren't much cop. There's the famous one of the Doctor and Romana pelting down the ship's exit before it detonates; other than that, there weren't that many good stock photos from that series. It meant I'd spend a day or so freeze-framing an old iffy VHS recording to get the right dimensions, angles, and colours. A time-consuming thing to do.

The reference of the Doctor and Romana is actually from the press call of Tom Baker and Lalla Ward's engagement announcement, hence his less Doctor-like expression. Maybe in retrospect I should have gone with a darker and moodier Tom and Lalla to fit the story. I simply thought it was a lovely piece to remember a fond, albeit brief, time for them both.

I really wanted to emphasise the sci-fi element in *Destiny of the Daleks* and so incorporated the space effect. Then there was this nice photo of Davros, which mostly black, so I just slightly picked out the detail of his mask. I thought it would be lovely to

use because the actual mask in the show looked a little bit ropey; it's a stretched-out original that was used again from *Genesis of the Daleks* to save money after the production team invested in Steadicam [camera stabiliser mounts] equipment.

Still, you have to pick out the details of the mask, so why not merge him with the space background and have him sort of there-but-not-there. Have Davros whispering away into the galaxy...

(*above*) *The published cover for* Destiny of the Daleks.
(*opposite*) *Original VHS artwork.*

DESTINY OF THE DALEKS (VHS)

TIMESLIDES: THE DOCTOR WHO ART OF COLIN HOWARD

THE SEEDS OF DOOM (VHS)

Starring the Fourth Doctor and Sarah Jane Smith. Released in August 1994.
"...the size of St Paul's Cathedral. After that, it will multiply itself a thousand fold until it takes over your entire planet."

Being keen on monsters, I used the Krynoid as my starting point on this. I decided to have the three stages of Krynoid evolution as my focal point, so there are the tendrils coming out of the pod at the bottom, going up into the re-sprayed Axon (from *The Claws of Axos*) in the middle, and then I tried to fade out the giant Krynoid mass behind. That was done from a freeze-frame too, looking at how the shoots moved as they came out of the pod, then translating that motion into the image.

The premise of *Seeds…* was very much like *The Thing* (1982), with the alien menace augmenting an unsuspecting scientist and slowly altering his recognisable human form into a shambling alien monstrosity. We lived in the countryside, so as a child, it was easy to imagine your pleasant leafy surroundings being possessed by an alien intelligence, trying to drag you into the ground and turn you into compost!

I really like the polar setting at the start of the story – that pale, icy, windswept snowy clime. I've airbrushed it here, and as I look at the effect now, it subconsciously merges into the split diamond of the Third Doctor's titles. I was trying to capture that encompassing blizzard, because I always really enjoyed the base-under-siege settings in twentieth-century *Doctor Who*.

I'd found this lovely picture of Elisabeth Sladen that I really wanted to use on a cover. That's what I always did: I'd make a note in the aforementioned litany of where images appeared and how I could access them in future, should I need them for work in *DWM* or fanzines. I typed it all out by hand and then bound it together myself – a very Heath Robinson approach!

It was incredibly handy to have a journal with all these reference photos listed, because it took away the laborious hours of leafing through piles of magazines, looking for specific things. This glossary of images was especially good with Tom's Doctor, recording which season the reference was from, and which costume featured. The grey jacket here lent itself to the snowy background. Then I used a purple tint because it went nicely with the green of the Krynoid.

As ever, the layering approach here would've started with the background, then working forwards, adding in those mountainous ridges. But you had to make sure it all flowed and didn't look like layers. The pod would've been the last thing I painted except, to make it work, I popped in a whizzing, snowy effect coming out from beneath it; this, along with the tendril feelers, overlap Tom's scarf, part of his cravat, and some of Liz's hair and costume.

It's interesting that I've kept some of the Axon's orange hues. It blends into Tom's hair quite nicely. I'd forgotten those fronds they stuck on the Krynoids' heads, to differentiate it from the original Axon costume. You tend not to notice much until you look closer at the creature itself. And I'd forgotten the massive amount of snow effect I sprayed on. You literally get a brush, make sure it's thickly loaded with paint, and flick it at the artwork. I used to do that with star fields too, in various colours.

(above) Original artwork for The Seeds of Doom.
(opposite) Original VHS artwork.

THE SEEDS OF DOOM (VHS)

TIMESLIDES: THE DOCTOR WHO ART OF COLIN HOWARD

KINDA (VHS)

Starring the Fifth Doctor, Tegan Jovanka, Nyssa, and Adric. Released in October 1994.
"It is the Mara who now turns the wheel. The Mara who dances to the music of our despair. Our suffering is the Mara's delight. Our madness the Mara's meat and drink. And now he has returned..."

This was a strange one to get your head around – simply to watch, let alone to try and come up with an image for. But I particularly like those sequences inside Tegan's mind with the actual Mara. I also love those theatrical Elizabethan-costumed creatures, although I couldn't really think of a way to easily work them into the image.

As usual, the eventual design resulted from time limitations and a lack of references, which I couldn't get hold of quickly enough. I would've liked to have had the main Mara featured in there somewhere, but instead I went for the chimes blending up into Peter Davison's jacket. Then I wanted to include the planet's surface a bit in the background, to give a bit more context and show off the jungle planet where the tribespeople were living.

I think even the Tegan reference that I used was actually from *The Visitation*. It was probably a black-and-white image from *Doctor Who Magazine* that I then had to paint in colour, which can be really difficult work.

Doctor Who Magazine was my Bible for most of these things, simply because they actually archived every story in the past. Often, I'd turn to whatever they printed – it could have been a heavily over or underexposed black-and-white image from however long ago, but that was frequently the only source of reference you would have.

Fans will have spotted the problem. It's exacerbated by the images on the back cover too. The Doctor's wearing the wrong jumper.

The Radio Times had released a special with a reference photo, I think from *Warriors of the Deep*, showing the Doctor, Tegan, and Turlough, issued as a poster. And I thought, "I love that reference picture of Peter; I want to use that one." That's often the way it is. As soon as you saw a brilliant new reference, you'd want to go with that. So that's what I did.

I still get the odd complaint: "The Doctor's in the wrong jumper – the one you've used is from Season 21 and *Kinda* is Season 19. How could you make that mistake?" It happens. He changes his shirt and there are differences in trouser patterns too. The jumper is just the most noticeable here, and I don't think it particularly impacts the cover.

I'm sure the celery is out of date as well.

(above) Original sketch for Kinda.
(above left) The printed VHS sleeve.
(opposite) Original VHS artwork.

KINDA (VHS)

TIMESLIDES: THE DOCTOR WHO ART OF COLIN HOWARD

SNAKEDANCE (VHS)

Starring the Fifth Doctor, Tegan Jovanka, and Nyssa. Released in December 1994.
"We're not supposed to be here…"

Even though they were released one after the other, I don't think *Kinda* and *Snakedance* were commissioned together. It was coincidental.

This was rather a nice serial though, one that I really liked from the Davison era, and I'm happy with how this cover turned out. Then again, I was always a sucker for the beautiful Nyssa. Sarah Sutton was in a play in Norwich years ago, and I managed to see her in that, which was lovely. But also it was great finding some fantastic pictures of both companions, of Janet and Sarah, and having the opportunity to reproduce those likenesses.

And I got to play with Peter's jacket – always a major bugbear with the Fifth Doctor. This mustard/ochre jacket really jarred with any kind of feeling that you wanted to get into a painting. Whatever you were going for, you always had to plunk in this vibrant, loud, shocking coat. So with this one, I merged it into some of the rocks, dragging some texture into the sleeve to the side of Janet's head, gradating the colour from the grey rock, up to those midtones, then up to the lighter tones of the Doctor's jacket.

The subtle, faded neighbouring planet on the horizon was to highlight that this is a science fiction show, set on other planets; it's not just somewhere on Earth or in a studio somewhere.

I was impressed with that snake-mouth cave opening as well, so I added these eerie, atmospheric wisps coming from it, hinting that something unpleasant might be lurking within.

I wanted the Mara to be unfurled, to look as threatening and realistic as possible. I know the snake here looked better than the puppet version from *Kinda*, but still I thought it needed a little help. That's why I made it a bit more glistening, and why you've got the venom streaming from its fangs.

I picked up a few snakes when I was volunteering at a conservation project in South Africa, which housed the big cats. There were puff adders and various cobras – two of the most venomous snakes there, but if you weren't careful, they'd poison the cats. I'd have to go into the cats' enclosures, clean out their cages and the lush, vegetated areas they stayed in, places with plenty of spots they could hide. Once I had to carry a constrictor in a bag on my back for a while, because we didn't want it to bite the cheetahs. A ranger just popped this snake into a bag and handed it to me!

That sort of stuff doesn't especially phase me, because I just love nature. It's fantastic to see it at close quarters, and you don't always have to travel far. I recently visited a big cat sanctuary near here and fed one of their Siberian tigers.

Mostly, you need respect and awareness. For instance, you have to be up-wind of a rhino, because if it smells you, and it's an aggressive male, it might decide to have a go. Know your surroundings and research the creatures that you might encounter, so you don't bumble around and end up a statistic.

SNAKEDANCE (VHS)

(left) Original sketch for Snakedance.
(below) Original VHS artwork.

TIMESLIDES: THE DOCTOR WHO ART OF COLIN HOWARD

THE ANDROID INVASION (VHS)

Starring the Fourth Doctor, Sarah Jane Smith, and Harry Sullivan. Released in March 1995.
"Is that finger loaded?"

Like everyone else, I have favourites of my own work, and *The Android Invasion* is one such piece. I've still got the original artwork for this one.

Reference photos were difficult, again, particularly for the Kraals. I had to have that picture of the Doctor tied to the monolith with two Androids behind him, almost like the burning of a witch. That conjured up the cover's tone and composition. But I made a rod for my own back.

The thing about Tom is, as much as I love his Doctor, there's: the hair, the fabrics, all the knitted bits, the scarf – all that detail! I had to add colour to the original reference photo, so I checked other stories from that time – *The Seeds of Doom*, particularly – to actually get the correct palette, and the right colour sequence for the scarf. That said, my favourite Doctor to draw is still Tom.

That led me to think about playing with light and dark. You've got the top of the monolith, which is quite dark; you put that against the centre of a wormhole-type effect, which is brighter, and it gives a nice juxtaposition with colour and with light levels.

As you're creating the design, you remember watching the story as a child. When the Android Sarah's face falls off, I was going, "Oh, God!" So I had to get that moment in as well. It was sketched from a freeze-frame of a wobbly old VHS. I think the details of the electronics were based on an on-file image of a Kraal scanner, so you're bringing in an added detail from the programme, and being a bit creative with it.

I also wanted Styggron glaring towards the Doctor, but the only photo of Styggron I could find was wrong. He was looking in the opposite direction to the way I needed. And of course, it was in black-and-white too.

I had that reference photo on my desk, placed a mirror in front of it, and sketched the reflection. Then I had to reimagine everything because I didn't have a photocopier, so I couldn't easily flip the image.

You had to rely on more desperate creative measures to get things done back then! Fortunately, it worked, and I think the end effect balances the piece off very nicely.

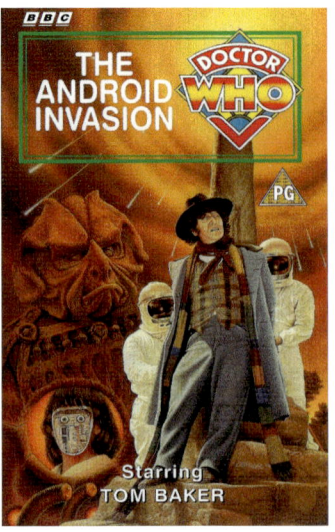

Unusually, on the back of the sleeve, where they'd typically include photos, the publishers used my cut up artwork, even the reversed Styggron. I think there are very few reference photos from that story and a lot were only in black-and-white.

(left) Original sketch for The Android Invasion.
(above) The printed VHS sleeve.
(opposite) Original VHS artwork.

THE ANDROID INVASION (VHS)

27

TIMESLIDES: THE DOCTOR WHO ART OF COLIN HOWARD

CARNIVAL OF MONSTERS (VHS)

Starring the Third Doctor and Jo Grant. Released in March 1995.
"Give them a hygiene chamber and they store fossil fuel in it."

I was lucky in that it was comparatively rare for notes to come back on my pencils, asking for me to change something. They must have liked what I supplied; it was very rare that I would have to change things for, say, *DWM*, and only the odd change here and there for the VHS covers.

If you look at the original pencil for *Carnival of Monsters*, it's a totally different Jon Pertwee reference photo from the one I ended up using, which came from *The Dæmons*. He was originally meant to be looking out towards the spine, at the same sort of angle as Vorg.

But I sent that sketch in and they said, "Could we have the Doctor looking more front-on instead?" I had to erase him and redraw a different Pertwee pose, which I didn't feel worked with the balance of the piece. But that's what had to be done to get approval. I don't believe I used that original pencil reference for anything else – I think it was from *Day of the Daleks*, where the Doctor is like this sunlit hero, looking to the side, which I thought would have worked brilliantly. I did manage to work it in to a private commission featuring a Sea Devil quite a few years later. It was too nice an image just to let go of, especially as he was my early childhood Doctor.

I also got to have some fun painting the Drashigs, a wonderful terror from my youth. I believe they were glove puppets, built around a fox's skull, but they had lovely detail, a bit like Mr Punch's crocodile – on steroids! In fact, they were a lot like the fantasy monsters from some of my favourite childhood films, stop motion animated or moving props. So I have a soft spot for the Drashigs and gave them top billing.

CARNIVAL OF MONSTERS (VHS)

(opposite left) The first version of Carnival of Monsters.
(opposite right) The approved Carnival of Monsters *sketch, with amended Jon Pertwee.*
(below) Original VHS artwork

TIMESLIDES: THE DOCTOR WHO ART OF COLIN HOWARD

THE RIBOS OPERATION (VHS)

Starring the Fourth Doctor, the First Romana and K9. Released in April 1995.
"My name is Romandveratnalundar."
"Well I'm sorry about that. Is there anything we can do?"

The *Key to Time* season was a bit of a pressure cooker because I was only given eight weeks to do all six covers, which were assigned together as a block. I was told not to worry about the linking spine art, as Andrew Skilleter was doing that, so I was just left with… the Doctor, wearing the most elaborate costume on TV, to paint intricately over and over again.

But it was a nice set of stories, and at least I also got to paint the lovely Mary Tamm every so often for a few weeks. She's in all of my Key to Time covers except *The Pirate Planet*; I hadn't really painted her very much at all previously, and why wouldn't you include her much as possible? Mary Tamm was a very beautiful woman, and companions are always a big part of *Doctor Who*. It was nice to give her a bit of a presence on the covers.

I did manage to see her once, at one of the *Doctor Who Appreciation Society* events – the Panopticon, I believe. I think Nick Briggs interviewed her. But I didn't, as usual, get to spend much time watching panels and those sorts of things: as an artist, you're lashed to the merchandise area, trying to sell enough wares to actually cover to the cost of the event! It was nice to get the chance to see her at least.

In the early days of going to conventions, I met Jon Pertwee, and he looked through my portfolio. He was very complimentary, which was simply amazing. He was my first real Doctor, and here he was, at a busy event, taking time out to look at my work, and saying what a good likeness of Roger Delgado I'd done! It meant a lot.

The most starstruck I think I've ever been is with Tom Baker. To actually meet your main childhood Doctor was phenomenal. This was shortly after I'd done the cover for the VHS, *Who On Earth Is Tom Baker?*, for Reeltime Pictures; he was doing a signing at Chapel-en-le-Frith. You forget what an incredibly imposing figure he cuts, what an intense gaze he has – it just gets into you, like being hypnotised! Chatting to Tom Baker… It was amazing. I felt inadequate and was garbling away so probably didn't make much sense, knowing me.

The Ribos Operation was, weirdly, one of my favourites from season sixteen.

I liked the concept of the crown jewels robbery, and that it's mostly a character-based piece with a very *Wizard of Oz* kind of castle. I tried to get that across on the cover.

And I particularly enjoyed the Unstoffe and Garron double act, which led to a few chortles. I really felt for Binro, the poor old guy that Unstoffe was hiding with, that dishevelled peasant in the shadows! I thought he was rather lovely. I always liked the pathos that Robert Holmes put into his characters. That was an important thing for me to get across on this cover, and I included Garron at the very least with the crystal incarnation of the Key segment.

THE RIBOS OPERATION (VHS)

(opposite right) Original sketch for The Ribos Operation.
(below) Original VHS artwork.

31

TIMESLIDES: THE DOCTOR WHO ART OF COLIN HOWARD

THE PIRATE PLANET (VHS)

Starring the Fourth Doctor, the First Romana and K9. Released in April 1995.
"Romana, we've stumbled upon one of the most heinous crimes ever committed in this galaxy."

When coming up with ideas, you're sat facing a blank sheet of card, and sometimes you think, "What the heck am I going to put on here?" You have to convey the story, and sometimes there are obvious choices to make. Other times it's far more complex. You don't want things to get too convoluted. "How the heck can I portray all these events, let alone find the references that I need?" But I found *The Pirate Planet* very easy to put together.

I think the reference for Tom Baker here was from *The Book Tower*, a programme he presented from 1979 to 1981. It was probably one of the publicity shots that he did, where he's just sat in a tweed suit or something. So I just popped him into his costume. It's like an early version of Photoshop.

Then you had to have the Pirate Captain and his citadel surrounded by guards. And of course, the pirate planet itself, which hopped around through space enveloping other planets! That's intrinsic. You have to feature that somehow.

It's quite a moody piece. I'm pleased with it. I've still got the original of this one. I think it all balances out and works pretty well.

Yet this was a story I was a little bit nervous about doing. Because for me, it doesn't have that much going on visually, other than what I've got on the canvas. Admittedly, there's the Mentiads, but then you have to do hordes of people looking a bit washed out, like *Doctor Who* fans after a marathon binge session.

You won't be surprised to read that I'm a Douglas Adams fan as well. Only he could really have come up with such a crazy idea as *The Pirate Planet*. Also, there's that wonderful relationship between the Captain and Mr Fibuli, with the remnants of Queen Xanxia pulling the strings through her puppet avatar.

On the sketch, you can see a note reading, "Dear Sarah [Andrews], Please allow 10- 15 minutes before phoning". That's because I'd draw a cover idea, tuck it under my arm, then head down to a store with a photocopier. That's one reason these are generally A3: most places only had A3 scanners! Then I'd reduce that to A4 so I could fax them to the BBC. I needed five minutes to get home before they could ring to approve or suggest alterations. I was fortunate that they almost always went with my first idea. The more you play around with stuff and incorporate too many ideas from other people, it becomes designed by committee, and you lose the original impact.

If they *did* need anything altering (as you saw with *Carnival of Monsters*), I'd amend the sketch, then repeat the trip to the local copiers. I'd then carefully package the artwork, cover the parcel in "FRAGILE" tape, and head off to the Post Office. This was my life until the death knell of traditional painted artworks and the dawn of computer design.

(left) original sketch for The Pirate Planet.
(opposite) Original VHS artwork.

THE PIRATE PLANET (VHS)

TIMESLIDES: THE DOCTOR WHO ART OF COLIN HOWARD

THE STONES OF BLOOD (VHS)

Starring the Fourth Doctor, the First Romana and K9. Released in May 1995.
"Doctor, did I understand you correctly: that thing is made from stone?"
"Yes, yes, and it's closing in on us fast."

You don't really see much of the Megara, so I wanted to give them a bit of cover space here as they're a nice, unusual "enemy" (even if they did get a little covered up by the *Doctor Who* logo on the VHS).

What was most important for me with *The Stones of Blood*, though, was having that wonderful Cailleach costume centre stage. It's a great design, very creepy, and works as a neat focal point.

It was a busy time because this was done on a conveyor belt: six paintings in eight weeks. Two months to put the whole of *The Key to Time* together (and it took the Doctor and Romana longer than that.) That was from scratch: all the pencils, getting approval, getting the right references and colour combinations, and everything else.

So this cover is me being an idiot and still chucking lots of elements into the picture. I was on a real deadline, under a lot of pressure… but I wanted to have the Cailleach in there, because it's such a nice costume.

And then there's those big, lumbering Ogri as well, the main threatening presence in the story. I wanted to have them looking as menacing as possible, looming out over the main characters.

My colour choices were largely to reflect how things were on screen. One of the most memorable bits in *The Stones of Blood* is the Ogri glowing from within, showing that molten aspect, pulsing as they moved. I wanted to get that across here, so I had their glow bookending either side. Then you needed a darker contrast at the top of the artwork.

Airbrushing like you see here is quite difficult to learn. Essentially, you're pointing a jet of paint and air onto your piece, so you're always trying to hone and refine the technique. Depending on the airbrush and the angle of impact, you can get it down to a fine point. But you have to use an incredibly solvent and runny milk-like paint mix. For me, I'd pick a colour palette that I wanted to work with, then start to spray in these mid-tones, down through to darker tones, to create clouds, stars, or a water effect, all depending on the story.

You have to smooth all that together, before adding even lighter tones to pull out detail and create a bit of atmosphere. You're essentially doing similarly to how you would with a brush, but you get a far smoother, nicer effect, which is especially important if you're doing space-related things. Saying that, I have produced a few pieces by hand with no airbrushing at all, and it *is* possible to get a similar effect with dry brushing.

Most of my paintings are in acrylic, with backgrounds sometimes thinned down with painting inks. If I wanted particularly rich tones, I would overspray the piece with painting inks afterwards, to bring more depth and warmth to the colours. In the early days, I used Gouache as well, which is more powdery and opaque, but harder to come by. When you're trying to keep a good stock of colours, it's better to get something that's more readily available. Acrylic dries quickly, enabling you to work in layers, adding new elements to those you've finished minutes before.

THE STONES OF BLOOD (VHS)

(opposite left) Original sketch for The Stones of Blood.
(below) Original VHS artwork.

35

TIMESLIDES: THE DOCTOR WHO ART OF COLIN HOWARD

THE ANDROIDS OF TARA (VHS)

Starring the Fourth Doctor, the First Romana and K9. Released in May 1995.
"Would you mind not standing on my chest? My hat's on fire."

I hadn't really done much with K9, so I made a concerted effort to get him on this one.

The Androids of Tara has a Brothers Grimm kind of feel to it. It's in that fairytale realm. I wanted to get that tone across, which is why you've got that citadel behind Count Grendel of Gracht. I like the baroque approach, so I had that intricate design at the top; even though I knew the title would go over it, some of the sets were so lavishly done that it was nice to bring that element to the front, again to properly represent the serial.

With this one, the main challenge was to take something that was essentially a stage play, in the best possible way, and to remind people that it still had all the trappings of a science fiction programme. You needed that gold work, that castle, the space backdrop, to show that it was a combination of the two, with Tom Baker bleeding off into the shadows at the bottom. And that scarf again! Aaargh!

As I say, Andrew Skilleter did the spine art for *The Key to Time* stories, and I think he was one of the first people I saw airbrushing. I admired his work on calendars, on *DWM*, and of course on book and video jackets, so I decided to teach myself how to use an airbrush too. That was really a product of the '80s and '90s. It was something we all seemed to learn at that time, and unfortunately, it seems to have died a death, I suppose with the advent of computers.

Then again, I think that's true of many traditional art techniques. What you see online is mostly stuff that's been done with various programmes on iPads, etc. That's something I *can* do, but I'd rather produce a painting, instead of tinkering around with photos or whatever.

Now and again, I would buy portfolio books of other great artists and study what they were doing, aspiring to learn how to create similar effects myself.

Sometimes, you can only do that with a vague prior understanding of how certain materials and mediums worked. With airbrushing, it's nice to keep a heavier pigment paint on hand, to do things like star effects and

ripples in water. You know it's going to retain its opaqueness and stay where it is, whereas if you keep trying with something that's far too diluted or translucent, it's not really going to give you that desired effect. It's going to muddy things. It's a case of trial and error, perseverance, trying different ways of doing things. But very few artists do things the same way if there's no formal training. It was only by reading books that you might hope to learn these things. There was no *Airbrush Along with Nancy*, no Bob Ross to show you what to do. You just had to work it out for yourself.

THE ANDROIDS OF TARA (VHS)

(opposite right) Original sketch for The Androids of Tara.
(below) Original VHS artwork.

TIMESLIDES: THE DOCTOR WHO ART OF COLIN HOWARD

THE POWER OF KROLL (VHS)

Starring the Fourth Doctor, the First Romana and K9. Released in June 1995.
"Oh, it's a Holy Writ."
"It's atrociously writ."

I'm still fond of this one because it's a lovely one of Mary Tamm. I decided early on that I wanted to do a one-colour portrait of her blended into a background, so *The Power of Kroll*, this watery world, gave me a good opportunity to do that. With Kroll himself, I wanted to add a bit more of the production team's original intention too: my focus was on having more tentacles and getting some movement into them – then to have one arching up, around, and over Romana, a bit like one of those old-style oval picture frames. That helps draw your attention to that portrait.

And oh no, it's Tom's hair and scarf again! I thought, 'What can I do to make my life easier here?' I knew the reed beds in the swamp were quite high so popping those in would, I thought, mean I didn't have to spend so much time painting the scarf.

That worked really well because instead, I had to do hundreds of reeds, bending and arching in different ways, catching the light…

It helps bring everything together though, and integrates the Doctor into the story's location, Delta III, with the threat being very visible behind him, and John Abineri's Ranquin lurking in the reeds as well.

The dad of one of my school friends was actually one of the Swampies. He was bussed in with a few other locals, painted green, and given these curious clothes just to run around this marshland in. My friend was obviously over the moon; I admit to tinges of jealousy. He quite happily told everyone; a bit of tittle-tattle around the village isn't going to spoil anything. It was rural East Anglia. Even the fastest horse with a messenger would take a while to get to civilisation to spread the news!

Not that I really went to filming locations anyway. I was just a kid at school, with working parents, so we didn't really have time to organise a trip there. If it were more local, I guess it would've been easier to pop along and make a nuisance of yourself, but I think *The Power of Kroll* happened to be a quick location shoot. When I got deeper into fandom, too, it was later in life, and I'd discovered these things called 'pubs' and 'concerts' and 'girls', and other stuff to occupy my mind.

But *Doctor Who* was always important to me. Unfortunately, a lot of my early collection bit the dust when I got married. I'd left stuff at home and the next thing I knew, they'd been disposed of. I took a lot with me, of course, but, for instance, my *War of the Daleks* board game was exterminated.

Similarly, I should have more tapes than I do. The BBC would send me copies of the videos I'd worked on. Unfortunately, I lost most of my VHSes in a house move, from the small city centre house Michelle and I got when we got married. I had to shift a lot of stuff from inside the house because it needed to be gutted and decorated. Quite a bit of it went into a garage, but it was a very leaky, cold, concrete place with an asbestos roof and steel girders. The latter dripped water down onto storage boxes, so the tapes themselves got mouldy and some of the sleeves got wet too.

THE POWER OF KROLL (VHS)

(opposite, bottom left) Original sketch for The Power of Kroll.
(below) Original VHS artwork.

TIMESLIDES: THE DOCTOR WHO ART OF COLIN HOWARD

THE ARMAGEDDON FACTOR (VHS)

Starring the Fourth Doctor, the First Romana and K9. Released in June 1995.
"You don't beg for peace, Princess. You win it."

The Armageddon Factor is one of my favourite stories of this season. I always liked the Shadow, as a concept and as a character, and thought he would have been a brilliant creature to bring back in the future. But he was also the most troublesome part of this cover.

There were no good photographs of the character – apart from maybe one in *DWM* of him sitting on his throne, and even there you couldn't make out any detail.

My art relies on detail, on getting up close to characters and finding the right textures, shapes – the shadows of the Shadow. And so this had to come from a paused fan club video recorded when *The Armageddon Factor* had been on TV. I paused, did a drawing of what I saw on the cover of one of my sketch pads, then made colour notes on the mask and the make up.

(Well, actually, it was probably an old Betamax; yes, I went that way. More compact, slightly better quality: a good combo for artists having to source images from lots of different serials.)

This was my chance to have Lalla Ward on the cover as well, this time as Princess Astra, and I managed to crowbar K9 in there alongside one of the mutant servants of the Shadow.

You can normally find decent enough reference material for the Doctor, so he's central to a lot of my designs, including here. As it turned out, there were a good few on set photos with Romana too, and I chose one incorporating the Atrios "eagle" design. As a sci-fi fan, you want to get the twin planets in there, then the Shadow's space station (a lovely design) hovering between Atrios and Zeos, symbolising his interfering with their plans. That struck a chord with me, which is probably why it's my favourite cover of season sixteen.

Like a lot of my work, *The Armageddon Factor* was cropped quite heavily for the cover itself, so it's good to have it on show properly here. I've still got the original painting for this. A lot of the time, with paintings I've sold, I've only really been able to keep a laser copy scan, which is always A3 in size. Often, the paintings would be taller than that, and it being pre-Photoshop days, you would simply lose some of the close-up intricacies. Laser copies take away layers of lighter tones too, so I've had to scan them again and enhance these ranges to make them at all print-worthy.

(above left) Original pencils for The Armageddon Factor.
(above) Original sketch of the Shadow, based on a paused videotape recording.
(opposite) Original VHS artwork.

THE ARMAGEDDON FACTOR (VHS)

TIMESLIDES: THE DOCTOR WHO ART OF COLIN HOWARD

THE MARK OF THE RANI (VHS)

Starring the Sixth Doctor and Peri Brown. Released in July 1995.
"He'd get dizzy if he tried to walk in a straight line."

The *Mark of the Rani* was a fun one to do though. Unusually for me, it was a bit of a historical piece. That was a welcome challenge, which is why I featured Stephenson's *Rocket* and the mine shaft in the background to get across the adventure's setting.

Of course, you had to have the Rani's console at the bottom because it was such a quantum leap in TARDIS design! And there's a clue that it's *her*

plan to take this chemical from the brain, which is why I also had that particular illustration above the console, to add some context and show what she was up to.

It's a rare Anthony Ainley portrait here too. By the time I came along to do the VHS covers, a lot of the really classic stories had gone, released already, and it was a case of simply doing whatever the BBC said was in the schedule next. So I wasn't given too many with the Master. I did get to paint him for *Survival* too, but Andrew Skilleter did *Logopolis* and *Castrovalva*, Ainley's real introductions as the Master (he was in *The Keeper of Traken* as well, but primarily as Tremas). I did get to do *Logopolis* later on, first as a standard commission, then Slow Dazzle ended up using it for their postcard set, as well as my *Pyramids of Mars*.

To be honest, you sometimes lose track of where your artwork appears. You work on so many different projects, and many are uncredited or only credited in tiny writing somewhere obscure; either way, people are unaware of what you've worked on. A lot of it is fill-in work anyway: "Can you adjust this and this?" For example, I worked on an Il Divo album cover, where they'd got a photograph of them in a classically Italian street and they needed me to edit out the more modern, technical stuff, anything that didn't belong in the era they were trying to evoke. Nowadays, you can do that sort of thing on a Google Pixel phone.

Then there was a Cliff Richard album, him and a pink Cadillac on a white background. My job was to add shadows and remove reflections of gravel in the chrome of the car. It jarred with the setting they wanted. For Simple Minds' *Big Music* (2014), they had a 3D model of a satellite of speakers; I had to add detail and make them look dirtier, more like they'd been used. They sound like little jobs, but they take a while to do.

I did get a Number One album! I suppose comparatively few have that claim to fame. It was Tony Christie's *Definitive Collection*, after "(Is This the Way to) Amarillo" topped the charts with Peter Kay. *Definitive Collection* spent two weeks as the UK Albums' Chart Number One in March/April 2005.

While working, I used to be a regular Radio 1 listener, but more recently, I've swapped that for either specific albums, Big Finish, or something with a comedic bent. *Jago and Litefoot* is a favourite range. *The Scarifyers* is absolutely brilliant, as is Paul Magrs' *Baker's End*.

THE MARK OF THE RANI (VHS)

(opposite left) Original sketch for The Mark of the Rani
(below) Original VHS artwork.

TIMESLIDES: THE DOCTOR WHO ART OF COLIN HOWARD

TIME AND THE RANI (VHS)

Starring the Seventh Doctor and Melanie Bush. Released in July 1995.
"You don't understand regeneration, Mel. It's a lottery and I've drawn the short plank."

This one had quite an interesting genesis. I'm from a fairly remote city, so I'm used to there not being a lot on. There was one particular store that I always used to visit to get my photocopies done and to buy art materials. In fact, I bought my Rotring airbrush and compressor from there. One day they were having an open day, and they asked me if I'd come along and do a live demo.

I was sitting in store working on this video cover, spraying the background and creating the vivid pink skyline, while people wandered around and pondered what I was doing. That was fun, channelling my inner Tony Hart.

Unlike, I think, much of the fandom, I was fond of the Tetraps, those wonderful, giant bats with four eyes, and it was nice to get the chance to paint one of them. They're an interesting design and idea for a monster. You've always got to look for fresh inspiration. At least I didn't go so far as hanging this one upside-down from the cave ceiling, reversing the image like they did on the Target cover.

I liked the setting too. The Rani's citadel was impressive, so I felt that was good to get in there alongside the ancient, stylised cave entrance where the Tetraps were living. For some bizarre reason, I reversed a question mark in the starlight-swirl effect next to the Rani. I guess because I was always thinking, "What am I going to do on this cover?" You risk ending up doing the same thing over and over, and it's nice to change things up a bit. Also, it was a way of developing another background effect, something a little different to what I'd been doing before.

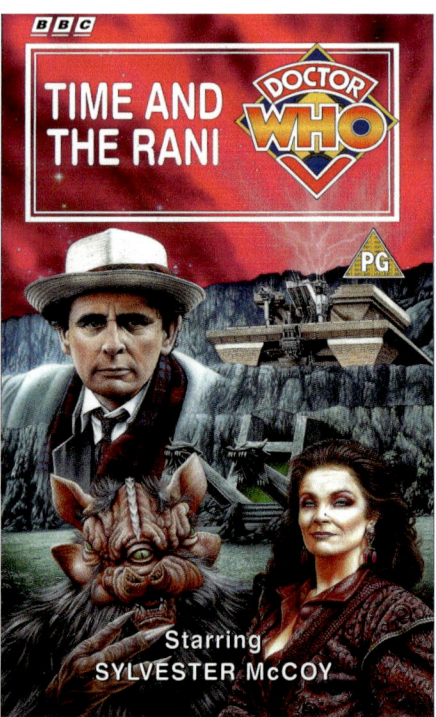

This was an intense cover. A lot of very finicky detail to play about with and get right. Sylvester's hat is a nightmare. It's this hand-woven straw hat, very textured and layered, with the Paisley scarf wrapped around it; you've got all that to do, then the same again with his tie. And the tartan scarf. You've got to recreate that exact pattern, and blend it in with the background. The jacket itself worked well, thanks to the grey rock-face behind, but to make the scarf segue nicely, you've got to work the rock up into the blue or grey checked scarf.

As ever, it was a pleasure to paint Kate O'Mara as the Rani, but here she's wearing a very heavily stylised, shiny, embroidered blouse, plus her surprisingly intricate earrings. It was a lot of fine work, but hopefully worth it.

TIME AND THE RANI (VHS)

(opposite left) Original sketch for Time and the Rani.
(opposite right) VHS cover.
(below) Original VHS artwork.

TIMESLIDES: THE DOCTOR WHO ART OF COLIN HOWARD

FRONTIER IN SPACE (VHS)

Starring the Third Doctor and Jo Grant. Released in August 1995.
"The treaty between our two empires established a frontier in space. We have never violated that frontier. You have invaded our part of the galaxy many times!"

It's good to achieve your goals, but your pride gets somewhat beaten out of you as a professional artist. You're constantly at the mercy of art directors and designers who don't like elements of what you do, who ask for changes or do overs. I was quite fortunate with the *Doctor Who* releases; I was rarely asked to change anything – although that might've had a lot to do with the fact that often the people commissioning me weren't really *Doctor Who* fans. They were normally fresh out of university, and it was just a nine-to-five job to them, which is fair enough. You'd put something together, and you'd know the fans would get it, but you just had to pray, "Please, God, let them like it!"

They always wanted me to make the show look as "sci-fi" as possible, to try and increase the appeal and tag it on with the contemporary popularity of things like *Star Trek: Deep Space Nine*. With *Doctor Who*, there were very few lavish space battles. It was stuff that had been filmed twenty or thirty years ago, and was always done on a budget. And so you then think, 'if I do all that, it's deceptive. You've got to represent the content of what the people are looking to buy.'

It's a bit like with the animations when I did the cover for *The Power of the Daleks*. I was not allowed to use photographic reference-based portraits of Doctor and companions, because it would be misrepresentative. You had to work only with what was visually there on the screen.

Still, I really enjoyed *Frontier in Space*. It was one of the few forays into an actual space war, the kind of thing I loved as a child. It felt related to things like *The War of the Worlds*. This was the period of the show that I first absolutely adored as a child – the era that really embedded *Doctor Who* in me.

It was nice to reimagine all those things that I loved as a child, and to pay homage to some fantastic Draconian masks by John Friedlander – quite a leap for *Doctor Who* as far as aliens went. Those high-end sculptures looked beautiful, and the Japanese-inspired costumes were great. I would have liked to have seen the Draconians return, because they were supposed to be the rivals of humanity at the time, which you'd think would earn you a bit more screen-time over the years. They were an absolutely brilliant creation.

And it was Pertwee, it was Delgado, it was the Daleks, and it was the great big grumpy Ogrons! It was a chance to pull them all together and bring in some of the great effect shots. You've got the Draconian cruiser as well as the Earth shuttle taking off from the penal colony, although a lot of that got chopped off for the VHS.

I've had occasional complaints from fans who were disappointed that the Daleks didn't really feature in *Frontier in Space*, apart from right at the end of the last episode. But this story features the Daleks; therefore, you've got to put them on there. It's to keep the people commissioning the artwork happy; they think, "This one features the Daleks, so this will sell well."

FRONTIER IN SPACE (VHS)

(opposite left) Original pencils for Frontier in Space.
(below) Original VHS artwork.

TIMESLIDES: THE DOCTOR WHO ART OF COLIN HOWARD

THE SEA DEVILS (VHS)

Starring the Third Doctor and Jo Grant. Released in September 1995.
"We have other colonies hidden round the world. We shall be the victors in the war against mankind!"

This is probably my favourite of all the VHS covers I did. I've refused to sell the original artwork on many occasions. *The Sea Devils* was one of the Target books that I read and reread, alongside *Doctor Who and the Cave Monsters*.

This cover was a labour of love. The detail required to faithfully capture those incredible John Friedlander Sea Devil heads (pretty faithfully resurrected for *Legend of the Sea Devils*) was quite staggering: there are three of our Homo Reptilia/Eocene cousins, so that's three sets of detailed scaly heads and those string vest costumes! Working my way from darker tones up to light, with three sets of vests to realise, layer upon layer… you can imagine how intense it was. I must have been mad.

I particularly identified with the Silurians because, even before *Doctor Who,* I was as a big fan of dinosaurs. I adored the idea that, once upon a time, a race of highly-intelligent reptiles ruled the planet. One of the first illustrations I had published in Peter Haining's *Key to Time* book featured the Silurians too: it was of a man, the grumpy ape on planet Earth, with a Silurian and a Sea Devil above, looking down with disdain.

There was just something captivating about them. They were supposed to be the custodians of this planet. They went off into hibernation, and they didn't appoint us to take over in their stead. Good thing too, because we're not doing the best of jobs.

I've kept quite a few of my originals – more so than most other artists who worked on the covers were able to, I think. I really would struggle to part with *The Sea Devils*. I managed to keep hold of *The Five Doctors* for quite some time, as that was another favourite, but I did eventually sell it a few years ago. Now and then, if you're not getting the work, then you need to make some nasty decisions.

These took so long to produce, and I remember most of them very fondly. It's always a bit of a wrench to part with a piece, but nicer when you know the collector is going to treasure it. I used to keep a log of where I sold them to, but thirty years later that record's long lost. Life gets in the way. You lose touch, you lose people's contact details. But it'd be lovely to hear from anybody who still has one, and especially if it's still as treasured as when I relinquished it.

(above) Original sketch for The Sea Devils.
(below) Illustration for Key to Time.
(opposite) Original VHS artwork.

THE SEA DEVILS (VHS)

TIMESLIDES: THE DOCTOR WHO ART OF COLIN HOWARD

WARRIORS OF THE DEEP (VHS)

Starring the Fifth Doctor, Tegan Jovanka, and Vislor Turlough. Released in September 1995.
"There should have been another way."

I was incredibly happy to be given the chance to do *Warriors of the Deep*. Like most *Doctor Who* fans of a certain age, when it was announced that the Silurians and Sea Devils were coming back, I was hugely excited. It'd been so long since *The Sea Devils*, and I had no real memory of watching *Doctor Who and the Silurians* as a child at all. I'm sure I must have seen it at some point, though. Either way, my idea of the Silurians would've come from *Doctor Who and the Cave Monsters* somehow, meaning their return in *Warriors of the Deep* had my imagination to live up to!

Needless to say, I was always going to have the Silurians and Sea Devils towards the forefront of this one, as the focal point of the image.

This was an interesting reference of Peter Davison. He's got a sorrowful, pensive expression, which linked well to the serial's ending, using Hexachromite gas to kill all the Silurians and Sea Devils on the base. I wasn't a big fan of many of the widely-used shots going around at that time; I wanted something sort of ethereal and engaging to work with. I was pleased, then, to find a couple of different photos I could use as the basis of the design, to have the Sea Devils and Silurians flanking the Doctor.

The Doctor's jacket was a bit of a gift here. The ochre goes well with the green, so you can graduate colours nicely. That all blended neatly into the airbrushed background, with these wispy effects, before moving down to the lovely *Stingray*-esque underwater base.

This was also a chance to show a little bit of the Silurians and Sea Devils' technology, with their little scout ship submersible tootling along in the background. Plus the Myrka, which was, of course, *indescribably amazing*. Ahem. And it presumably gave some out-of-work actors something to do.

I liked the samurai look for the Sea Devils. They're *warriors* of the deep! With the story being set in the future, it took an interesting angle, revealing the bodies of the Sea Devils to be showing signs of decay because they've been hibernating for so long.

The redesign of the Silurian triad worked nicely too. The new heads were interesting – it was good to have a little bit of a carapace over them; this bony bodywork to protect them, taking inspiration from tortoises and giving them armour, which was an improvement on the more vulnerable looks of the original Silurians.

Most of these costumes having been created with latex and rubber, over time they too have decayed. I've had quite a few nice chats with Neil Cole of the Museum of Classic Sci-Fi, in Allendale. He's a lovely guy, who does a lot of painstaking repair work on these things… when he can actually get hold of them. It's very difficult to acquire originals of any note. You might be able to get the odd little scrap of something here and there, but an original screen-used monster costume is often way too expensive and difficult to find.

(left) Original pencils for Warriors of the Deep.
(opposite) Original VHS artwork.

WARRIORS OF THE DEEP (VHS)

TIMESLIDES: THE DOCTOR WHO ART OF COLIN HOWARD

PARADISE TOWERS (VHS)

Starring the Seventh Doctor and Melanie Bush. Released in October 1995.
"A visitor? Well, it must be a long time since the Tower saw any of those."

This one was quite a difficult one to come up with an idea for. It railed against everything that I was ever asked to do by the editors at the BBC, which was always to make *Doctor Who* appear space-orientated and full of action, which, in truth, it rarely was. *Paradise Towers* is sort of like *Doctor Who* as a weekly sitcom, just with these amazing robot cleaners. I really struggled with how I was going to come up with something vibrant and energetic but I was saved by the *Radio Times*.

It had a feature on *Paradise Towers*, and that's where the main reference comes from. They staged this photoshoot with Sylvester and Bonnie on the set, struggling with the pool cleaner robot. And I thought, "I've got to use that. That's putting action and dynamism at the centre of the composition." Then I added the main cleaner robot behind, chucking a gas cloud out and whirling its drill, plus Richard Briers' Chief Caretaker to the right.

You're always trying to work out how to make the design punchy and keep all the elements both distinct and well balanced. It's nice to have a very similar branded look to your covers, but then they do just all blur into one. Some art directors wanted them to be like the *Star Trek: Deep Space Nine* covers, but they were all dull and samey. You need something different, something vibrant, once in a while; I wanted to produce something that made people look twice, to stop in their tracks and soak it in.

The original is a tall, narrow A3, and you really have to refine your brushwork to be able to create a likeness that small. Bonnie and Sylvester's faces are about the size of your fingertip, slightly smaller than that, but to get an exciting composition you can't have a close-up portrait. It's got to be small. So you practise and practise, using finer and finer brushes. More recently, I used an adjustable magnifying glass arm to help create a heavily detailed, fine portrait at small scale. I now wear glasses, and I think that's probably due to eye strain, getting up close to these pieces.

This is one of the few paintings where my Cantonese signature is a bit more prominent on the painting: near the pool, to the left of Bonnie, and in red.

Michelle lived in Hong Kong in her early teens; her father worked out there. As a result, we've been out there a couple of times. One year, Michelle's mother gave me a gift of a Cantonese writing set: a pointed brush, an ink block, and a name stamp in Cantonese. Well, like visitors who get a tattoo while in the Far East, we're *told* it says "Colin", but it might read something completely different…

A lot of work around that time featured artists' signatures and guest initials, which is why I decided to change my standard signature to something to make people scratch their head, and think, "Oh, has he been replaced?" When I started doing it, Sarah Andrews at the BBC was contacted by someone who wanted to buy an original piece and was checking it was actually by me; Sarah told them, "I think he's signing his work in Gallifreyan now!"

(left) Original sketch for Paradise Towers.
(opposite) Original VHS artwork.

PARADISE TOWERS (VHS)

TIMESLIDES: THE DOCTOR WHO ART OF COLIN HOWARD

SURVIVAL (VHS)

Starring the Seventh Doctor and Ace. Released in October 1995.
"Life's not a game. I'm teaching you the art of survival – I'm teaching you to fight back."

Survival is my very own missing story. It was a massive shock at the time: you send your artwork away, and somewhere between the printers and the BBC, somebody thinks, "I'll have that, thank you very much." You're told it's gone walkies and you will probably never see it again, no matter how many appeals you make (believe me, I did try) to see it returned. It's probably framed on a fan's wall, or more likely forgotten about in a cupboard.

This version is a combination of a colour copy that I took at the time and the VHS cover, scanned and blown up and merged together, then digitally touched up a little by hand, to actually get the detail back again.

It's a real shame it never saw the light of day at the time, because I rather like it. I am a cat person. My wife and I worked in South Africa on a cheetah conservation programme for a little while, just before my MS kicked in, and we used to go on walks, training young cheetah

to hunt.

I'm a natural history nut and love wildlife – except for the way my particular species is treating the planet at the moment, of course. Cheetahs have an especially hard time in nature because they are so fragile and cannot risk injury, because if they get injured, they can't hunt. Lions hang out in prides and have large groups – indeed, most other cats are far more sociable – but cheetahs tend to be very individual and not that gregarious. And they can be bullied off their kills by animals like hyena, which just prowl around looking for a free meal; they can go to all the effort of bringing something down and then lose it within minutes.

For the conservation programme, you'd have to get up very early in the morning, walk for miles with them until they picked up the scent of something, then watch and wait while they went in for the kill. You'd have to keep an eye on them, find where they brought the prey down, and then wrestle it away from them because otherwise they'd gorge themselves and wouldn't be able to move for three hours. Unfortunately, you'd then have to pick up the kill and carry it back over your shoulder to keep the cats following and not

(left) Michelle and me with Khanya.
(above) Michelle and I pose with my marker pen graffiti on the wall of the conservation centre games room.
(opposite) Original pencils for Survival.

SURVIVAL (VHS)

55

TIMESLIDES: THE DOCTOR WHO ART OF COLIN HOWARD

just gorging and sleeping. After some butchery (some had to be dissected by myself), the prey would go in the cold room for storage, for those days when the cheetahs wouldn't be able to hunt. When you start to look into nature, you can easily understand the struggles. There are prey animals, there are predators, and that is the way of things. One's essential for the other. I can identify with Karra and the hunt.

One of the best memories I have was the first time we went out on a hunt with one of the big cats. A cheetah came over, started rubbing against me and purring. People don't often realise that cheetah do actually purr. These were orphaned cubs, so they were half tame, but still, at the end of the day, a wild animal – just one you felt a little bit safer with.

It was a great experience, digging irrigation ditches and taking down the structures for other enclosures. You'd go into an enclosure and there'd be cobras waiting for you, or a serval, or you'd have to enter the hyena pens to retrieve their leftovers.

Leaving the project was probably the most difficult thing we ever did as a couple. We were both in floods of tears because it was such a unique experience. I did a full marker-pen cheetah on the wall of the games room there as a parting gift. A bit of graffiti.

That's what makes *Survival* so poignant for me. Cheetahs, and especially the cubs, have the most beautiful faces, like something you'd see in the toy shop for little children. They are adorable.

I know some artists struggle with drawing animals, but when I'm not doing sci-fi stuff, I love to paint nature. The more interesting, the better. And *Survival* was a good one to do because you had the old school horror movie look for the Master, with his fangs in, and Sylvester with the skull. It's quite a dynamic piece, adding in the planet destroying itself, which wasn't shown on screen from that POV, blended with the lovely Sophie's iconic look – those contact lenses!

(left) Up close with Buhle.
(bottom left) Jabari rehydrates.
(above) Magazine advert for the VHS range – solely featuring my covers!
(opposite) Original VHS artwork.

SURVIVAL (VHS)

57

TIMESLIDES: THE DOCTOR WHO ART OF COLIN HOWARD

THE KING'S DEMONS (VHS)

Starring the Fifth Doctor, Tegan Jovanka, Vislor Turlough, and Kamelion.
Released in November 1995.
"We sing in praise of total war; against the Saracen we abhor."

The King's Demons and The Five Doctors came in a black twin box set together, which also had an album to put postcards in; the BBC had started popping the postcards of the covers in with each release. I've still got the box and the cards. Over time, as the releases came out, I put one of each in the plastic pockets for safekeeping. All but one are mine, from Frontier in Space to The Hand of Fear, plus Andrew Skilleter's K9 & Company.

Funnily enough, their numbering system didn't quite tally up. The Sea Devils is "Collectors' Card No. 3" and Warriors of the Deep is number 4. Paradise Towers is number 5; 6 is Survival; The Five Doctors, ironically, is 7, with, oddly, The King's Demons coming after it at number 8.

I obviously tried to put these in order at some point, but I missed the first two (one of which was my own Frontier in Space), meaning the set concludes with The Monster of Peladon (9) and The Hand of Fear (10).

A few of my artworks have been turned into postcards over the years. Slow Dazzle, a company I did a calendar for in 1999, decided to issue a set of postcards which were mostly my VHS covers – Inferno, The Android Invasion, The Mark of the Rani, and a few more, including some that had been used for the BBC's set, like Frontier in Space and The Sea Devils. The other pieces I had first done for the calendar, for example The Tenth Planet, The Evil of the Daleks, The Three Doctors, Logopolis, and The TV Movie.

Some of my collection was wrecked by damp. But I kept these – The King's Demons and The Five Doctors – along with The Sea Devils, The Armageddon Factor, and The Leisure Hive; those VHSes survived because they were kept inside, not banished to the cold wasteland outside.

It's a shame that the cover of The King's Demons was covered up by a box, because it pops out nicely. It was a Master versus Doctor adventure, and I was trying to find a way to give some visual dynamism to that. I wanted Kamelion in the centre because he was pivotal to the whole thing, with Gerald Flood as King John at the top.

The unusual composition mixed with the striking colours was a way to do something a bit different, to make this cover more vibrant and sci-fi, rather than just another period piece. It's quite a grounded, tight affair otherwise.

THE KING'S DEMONS (VHS)

(opposite left) The VHSes, slipcase, postcards, and folder for The King's Demons *and* The Five Doctors.
(opposite right) Original sketch for The King's Demons
(below) Original VHS artwork.

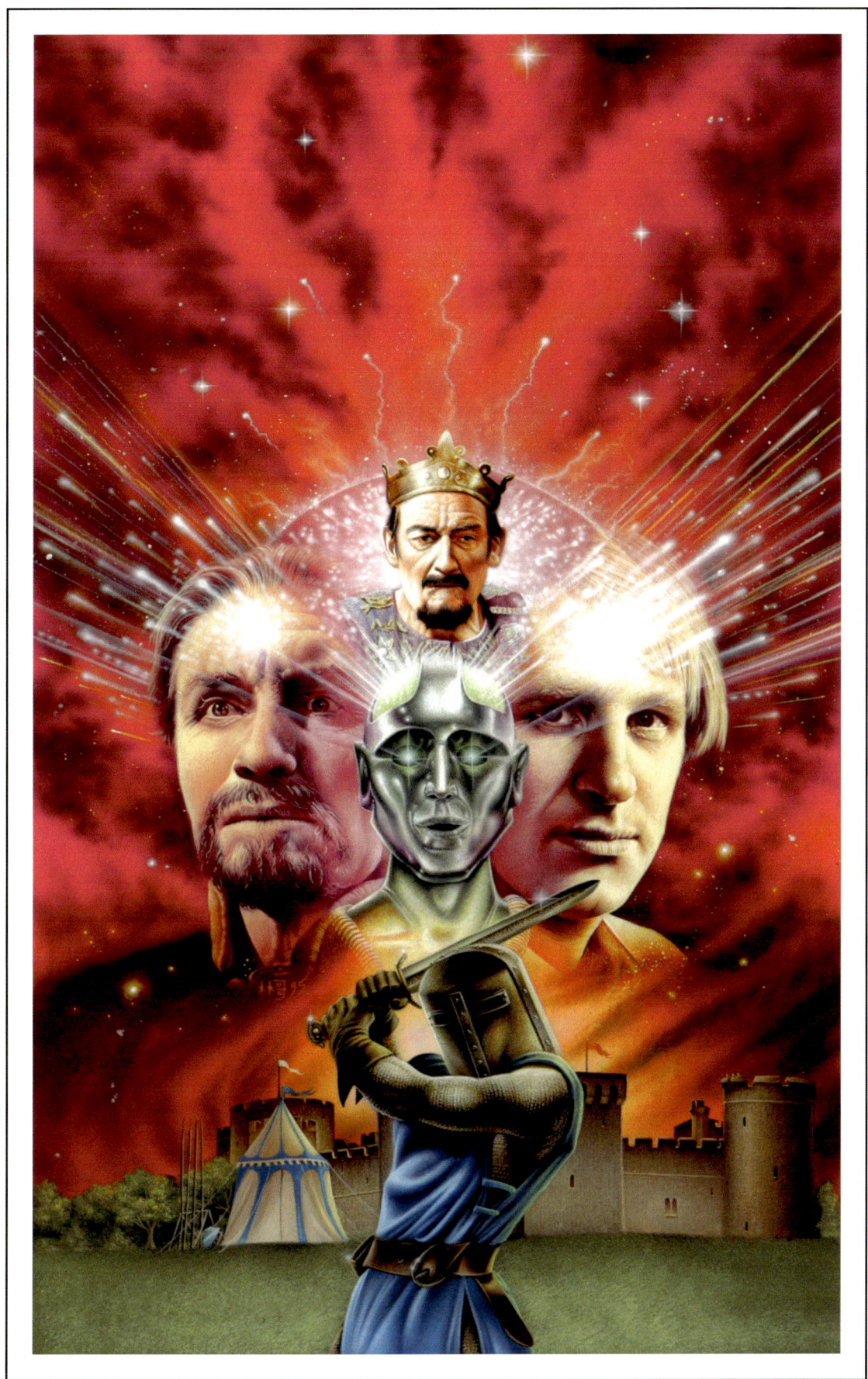

TIMESLIDES: THE DOCTOR WHO ART OF COLIN HOWARD

THE FIVE DOCTORS (VHS)

Starring the First, Second, Third, Fourth, and Fifth Doctors. Released in November 1995.
"I am being diminished, whittled away piece by piece. A man is the sum of his memories, you know, a Time Lord even more so…"

This is quite a punchy piece, and I think probably the one that suffered most at the hands of the printers and cover designers. Especially over the subsequent years, because apparently it was also the first DVD release. I wasn't even told it was being released on DVD. I never received a copy of it, let alone payment for reuse of my artwork, which was a bit poor.

It's really quite humbling when you have to go out and buy a copy of a product with your own art on.

There was a lot of *Five Doctors* art going around at the time, including the great *Radio Times* cover by Andrew Skilleter. I was trying to do something different, rather than the usual group of five Doctors' faces. I thought, "Essentially it's the Fifth Doctor's story because it's in his era. Is there a way I can include the others but less prominently?" I figured I'd do them in a red and yellow tone, rather than full colour; that way, Peter punches out more from the cover.

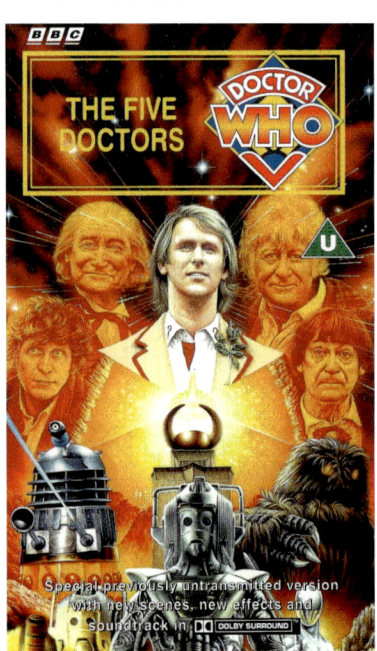

It's a sprawling story, so I came up with using Borusa's model chessboard as a template; that's in the middle, with its hexagonal shape as the basis for the centre point of the illustration. Then you've got that booming dark tower rising from it, and the other monsters arranged around there.

My great love of the Cybermen resulted in that nice mid-shot of one of them, and it seemed churlish not to have another exploding, impaled by the Raston Warrior robot firing a lance from behind. Then there were the Yeti, another creation that I loved. And of course, you can't do it without bringing in the Daleks, tempted as I was to go with the destroyed version with his tentacles hanging out.

The creatures essentially mirror the Doctors above. The Yeti reflects the Second Doctor; the Dalek reflects the Fourth Doctor; and you've got the Cybermen and Raston Warrior reflecting the triptych of Doctors One, Three, and Five. In my mind, it means they get equal billing.

You might notice the Raston Warrior's improved physique. Artistic license. Weirdly, no one's ever complained about that over the years. Put the wrong jumper on Peter Davison; you'll hear about it. Make the Raston Warrior robot a bit ripped? No one worries about that at all.

THE FIVE DOCTORS (VHS)

(opposite right) Original sketch for The Five Doctors.
(opposite left) The cropped VHS sleeve. The poor Raston Warrior spent weeks in the gym for nothing!
(below) Original VHS artwork.

TIMESLIDES: THE DOCTOR WHO ART OF COLIN HOWARD

THE MONSTER OF PELADON (VHS)

Starring the Third Doctor and Sarah Jane Smith. Released in December 1995.
"They go in for rough justice here on Peladon. Chop off your head and apologise afterwards."

Ah, Peladon. It was a setting I loved as a kid. For *The Monster of Peladon*, it was a case of deciding what to include. There are so many strong elements. I wanted to get my favourites in there but also make it a nice composition that flowed; otherwise, you're trying to over-egg it, chuck too much into a piece, and it ends up a hodgepodge that doesn't really sit well.

This is the only time I got to paint the Ice Warriors for the VHS range, and they're another creature I absolutely adored as a child. I thought they looked amazing, these giant, rampaging, tank-like creatures – very strange and frightening. Here, the positioning of the Ice Lord a bit further down, looming menacingly above the Citadel to hint at his intentions, helps offset the Doctor on the left, as if they're squaring to fight.

I felt I couldn't paint the "real" Aggedor because he only makes a rather fleeting appearance. But there was that statue at the temple, of Aggedor in an archway; I figured I'd go with that as the central point of the image itself, then have him flanked by an Ice Warrior and Alpha Centauri, who I opted to fade away into the background. I picked up some of the purples from the Citadel walls, which complemented Alpha Centauri's skin colour, and helped Jon's Doctor stand out a little more than if I'd just carried on with that green. Then I balanced that side of the composition with the Ice Warriors forming this nice "U" shape.

I first met Sadie Miller, Elisabeth Sladen's daughter, at the Capitol convention in 2022. I so would have loved to have shown her the original painting, but I had parted with it years previously.

There was a reason I wanted to show Sadie this specific cover. I'd met Lis back when I was working on the VHSes. I was at a *DWM* party at this little upstairs bar, and there were quite a few lovely celebrity guests there. I was itching to have a chat with Lis because she was my favourite childhood companion, the one I grew up with more than any other. And she was an incredibly warm lady. I was so happy and taken with how nice she was. We were chatting about her life and she mentioned that her little girl had started watching *Doctor Who* and loved seeing her mum on screen. So I said to her, "The next chance I get to do your portrait, I'll pop Sadie's name on the cover for you." And there it is, on Sarah's jacket!

More recently, I asked Sadie if she'd seen her name on the cover, and she was unaware of it. She might've been told about it as a child and had understandably forgotten. She went to the shelf and grabbed the tape – she still kept some of them, remarkably. You hope that that tie-in merchandise like that might be kept, no matter if it's locked in a box somewhere. You hope that people will be happy that somebody painted their portrait, took that time, showed that respect. So it was wonderful to know Sadie still had them.

She was amazed that she'd never really noticed it, that it had been there all these years. It was fantastic to get to meet her. She's a lovely lady as well, just like her mum.

THE MONSTER OF PELADON (VHS)

(opposite left) Original sketch for The Monster of Peladon.
(below) Original VHS artwork.

TIMESLIDES: THE DOCTOR WHO ART OF COLIN HOWARD

THE HAND OF FEAR (VHS)

Starring the Fourth Doctor and Sarah Jane Smith. Released in February 1996.
"Eldrad must live!"

I have strong memories of watching *The Hand of Fear* as a child. My most impressionable *Doctor Who* years began during the latter era of Jon Pertwee, and went on into Tom Baker's tenure. I fondly remember Sarah Jane. It meant a lot to actually produce this one, and it remains one of my favourites.

I particularly rate Judith Paris' Eldrad; she was excellent. I had to tactfully pause my old VHS tape to get Stephen Thorne's Eldrad in there too. I also like the idea of this desolate, windswept planet surface, with nothing apart from this dome – the sheer destruction that the planet had gone through because of Eldrad. This is one of the few that had exterior elements incorporated into the design. I didn't get to do the VHS cover for *Pyramids of Mars* (although I did revisit it for Slow Dazzle's calendar), but if I had, I would probably have looked at the landscapes and architecture a bit more.

It was nice to play around with the crystalline block textures, particularly on the hand fossil with its finger snapped off, and the female Eldrad's costume, with its intricate jewel patterning amongst the rocks. There's a lot of stippling and dry brushing going on there, to get the rocks right, as well as the smoother, nebulous airbrushing at the top.

When you're facing a blank sheet of card, you have to think, "How am I going to accurately convey this story? What are the most important things to prioritise?" Sometimes it's quite easy and there are obvious choices to make. Other times it's far more complex and convoluted. Still, working through which elements to include is the natural next step from whatever immediately comes to mind. Soon you've worked out your ideal design, and then it's down to your ability to transcribe what's in your head onto the card in front of you.

With most of my cover artworks, I'll have ideas of sympathetic elements from the off. For example, I was able to provide some nice contrast here with the image of the Kastrian Dome, which is very starkly lit in the foreground, surrounded by a lot of shadow and jagged rock structures. It's fun to play with that and blend different textures together.

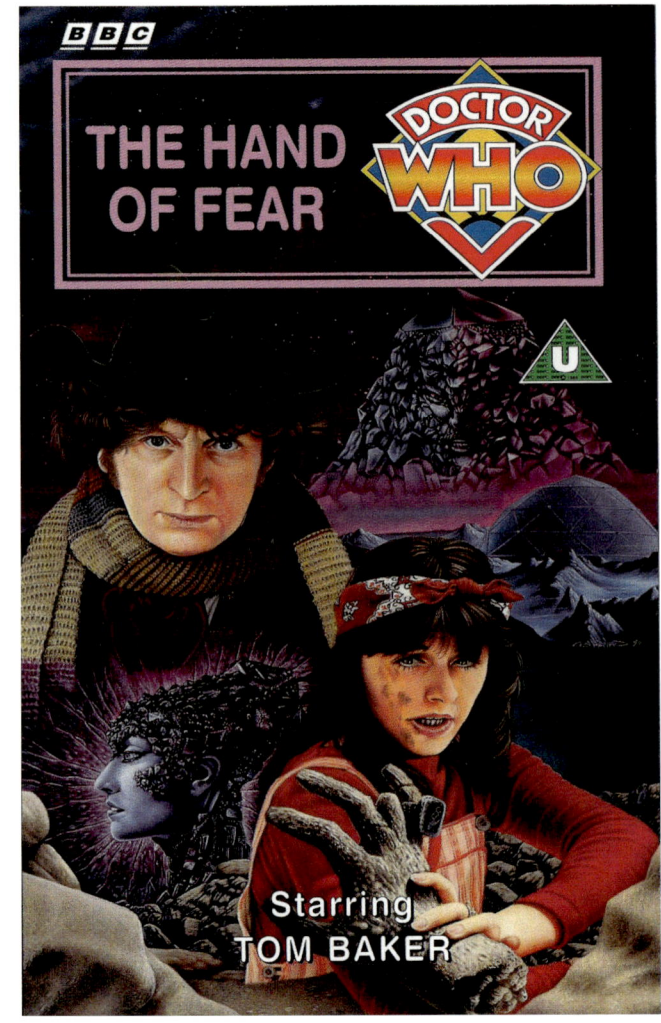

(top left) The printed VHS sleeve. (bottom left) My 1988 illustration of The Brain of Morbius *similarly put Sarah front and centre. (opposite) Original VHS artwork*

THE HAND OF FEAR (VHS)

TIMESLIDES: THE DOCTOR WHO ART OF COLIN HOWARD

THE LEISURE HIVE (VHS)

Starring the Fourth Doctor, the Second Romana and K9. Released in January 1997.
"I don't think much of this Earth idea of recreation. Why can't we do something constructive?"

I had fun making the exterior of Argolis look inhospitable, with that particular angle, the wind effect, and the lighting in the sky setting the mood for the piece. It's a nice moody Tom too. I felt that look fitted really well with the overall look of the cover – and the fact that it was his last season. Good to give him a more sombre air.

The Doctor's new costume for this season was an interesting evolution of the concept, though I'm not sure I would have gone with the maroon. As an artist, the trouble with that sort of colour palette is that the reds are difficult to get right and then to overlay, because they tend to be more translucent than opaque. If you're trying to pick out detail in a scarf, you need to have more of an opaque paint that will retain its form, to actually build up texture, rather than just melt down into what's there and add a darker tone. It was a struggle to get carmine reds and alizarin crimsons that would help lift out all the knitted detail of that scarf.

For *The Leisure Hive*, I had the background merging with his scarf, the lighting rising into the first fold of the scarf layer, and some of the surrounding colours reflecting in Tom's hair. Then the piece naturally moves forward to take in the Foamasi.

There's a lot of repeated detail work on the costumes. You have to look at the lighting that's involved in what you're doing and then opt for a mid-tone colour. A lot of the Foamasi is almost brown, heading towards gold, and then the greens come in. You try to merge all these colours together to create the texture and the depth in the skin/fabric, and then to keep the scale layers accurate (i.e. roughly the same size), retaining the same patterning, and linking. You have to account for the folds there as well.

You then build it all forwards, bringing these colours through, up to the lighter tones. I always work up towards almost pure white with my paintings. It means lots and lots of painstakingly intricate touching up of things that you've already painted over five, maybe six times, enhancing that and giving more depth to the piece. That's why, with most of my pieces, if you really look at them closely, you will struggle to see brush marks. In later life, as my painting improved and got better, I was able to get things to a near-photographic standard.

God bless reptilian creatures, eh?

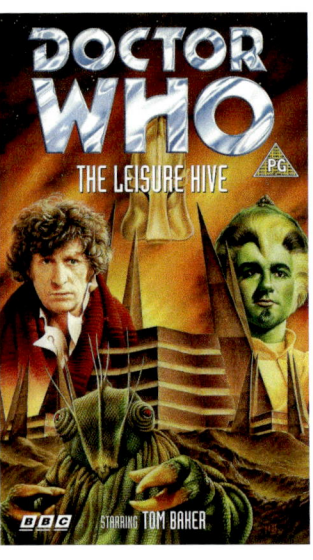

(left) Original sketch for The Leisure Hive. (right) The printed VHS. A new year and a new sleeve design (with my art on the spine too!) (opposite) Original VHS artwork.

THE LEISURE HIVE (VHS)

67

TIMESLIDES: THE DOCTOR WHO ART OF COLIN HOWARD

THE AWAKENING & FRONTIOS (VHS)

Starring the Fifth Doctor, Tegan Jovanka, and Vislor Turlough. Released in March 1997.
"I've got this one cheap because the walk's not quite right and then there's the accent."

This was my only double-release, where I had to bring two stories together. I was able to combine *The Awakening* and *Frontios* pretty well by using the idea of the broken church wall with the Malus, working in with Peter Davison's coat and the body of the Tractator as well.

It was a fairly easy to do because you've got a nice visual that you can focus in on and use as the basis for your layout. That's the good thing about the Malus breaking through the church wall – a wall is basically a canvas, so therefore you can find ways to incorporate that into the bigger composition.

There's a lot of added texture here, notably on the Malus and Gravis. The monsters are intrinsic to *Doctor Who*. Yes, great leading men, women, and supporting cast, but for me, it's the monsters. That was always my main draw, all the bizarre creatures. I liked to be scared as a child.

It could be quite a challenge to get good likenesses, especially with the typically short time constraints we were given. I saw that photo of Peter when I was planning; I don't think I'd seen it before – which is a rarity when it comes to reference pictures – so I had to include it.

This is one I'm very happy with. I've still got the original. I think all the likenesses are there and the general design of it is strong, having the Tractator globules in the darker background areas behind the Doctor. Between him and the Gravis, that organic hive-like element creeps in, to add to the alienness of the piece, plus you've got the crashed spaceship prop in the background.

I was always into my arts and crafts, not just painting. I had a lot of Airfix kits and various models; I even whittled myself a Sontaran out of balsa wood. When I was a kid, I made a little TARDIS console room diorama: my sister had a toy lipstick and so I thought, 'That's a time rotor,' then the console itself was polystyrene. I also used polystyrene to make K9, then put drawing pins in the base, so I was able to move him around the console with a magnet from underneath.

The things you do as a child!

I actually made myself a Sontaran costume in the late '80s, and it made the cover of the local newspaper. When we held conventions, our *Doctor Who* group would wander around the streets, drumming up interest. We did one in 1988, and I made myself a papier-mâché Sontaran head, bandaged my fingers together to make the right gloves, and added the collar.

I spent so long after school trying desperately to be an artist and not getting a lot of work, and I ended up as a community gardener for a year. People thought I was a convict, doing my penance, serving my time. There, I worked with another *Doctor Who* fan – a tall fella, fairly broad, so I made him an Ice Warrior costume. The headpiece was papier-mâché, but the actual body was chicken wire and glass fibre repair kits intended for cars.

I've always had quite a creative bent, and would have loved to have gone into TV prosthetics. I think it was a case of being born either too early or too late.

(left) Original pencils for The Awakening & Frontios.
(opposite) Original VHS artwork.

THE AWAKENING & FRONTIOS (VHS)

TIMESLIDES: THE DOCTOR WHO ART OF COLIN HOWARD

THE HAPPINESS PATROL (VHS)

Starring the Seventh Doctor and Ace. Released in August 1997.
"Have a nice death!"

The VHS cover might look entirely like a photo montage, but it's not. My art was partially used.

I was commissioned to paint *The Happiness Patrol*, and so I did the design, which was approved at pencil stage. I painted the full thing, and popped a pink TARDIS on there as well – that would've been a first, having that featured so heavily in that way. I did a lovely Kandy Man… and he ended up being the only thing that was used. They cut around the image of the Kandy Man and stuck him in a wonderful swirl and wider photo montage by design house Black Sheep Studios. At least it credits me on the back cover.

Designers on computers do things in a specific way, and that's how everyone wants their product to look, to fit in. That's great in its own way, but it's no good if it monopolises everything. You lose diversity. It's been like that for years. Lee Binding changed things with his covers. He's a lovely guy, and he basically assembles photographs in a way that creates a new composition and then enhances them by hand. You end up with a similar effect to what I get now, i.e. a digital painting that looks as though it's been painted, rather than a cobbled-together photo montage. It's actually painted, just on a graphics tablet, which is basically what I ended up doing with agencies after the video work and trade for traditional art dried up. You had to evolve or die.

I love the manic idea behind the Kandy Man. I did the interior pipe tunnel behind, with the fondant dribbling down and forming stalactites, and worked in some of the other patterns that were used on set. I liked the theatrical AmDram-style steps with the palm trees, giving a reflection of this bizarre land that the TARDIS has landed on.

Plus, this is one of my favourite Sylvester McCoy paintings that I did for the range, so it was a shame it got nixed.

There were a lot of good textures to play with in there, which led on to other things in later life; I'm now credited for digital background textures for some animations, notably *The Evil of the Daleks*.

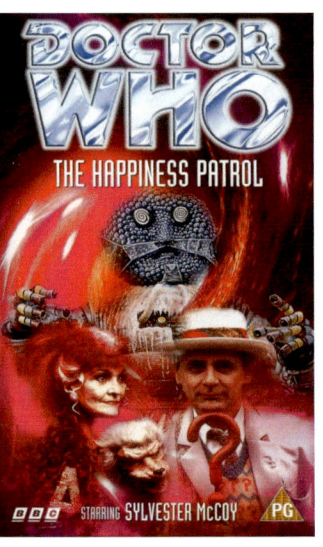

(far left) Original sketch for The Happiness Patrol. *(left) The actual VHS sleeve. (opposite) Original artwork, not released.*

THE HAPPINESS PATROL (VHS)

TIMESLIDES: THE DOCTOR WHO ART OF COLIN HOWARD

REVELATION OF THE DALEKS (VHS)

Starring the Sixth Doctor and Peri Brown.
Never released, although a 1999 VHS was issued in a special Dalek tin, paired with *Planet of the Daleks*, with photographic covers by Black Sheep.
"America doesn't have a monopoly on bad taste."

This was the one I finished just in time to get away for our much-belated honeymoon.

I painted *Revelation of the Daleks*, ready to go away, but I was told four days before I was due to fly that, instead, *Inferno* was required. This was only a week before *Revelation* was allocated for release. I believe it was something to do with the music licenses. The DJ popped out all those tunes, and that scuppered its release at the last minute. Clearances must've been a headache, so I guess that's why it was delayed after that, and why I only had a brief time to produce *Inferno*, from concept to final art.

I was very disappointed in the end when this one didn't see the light of day. A great shame.

As with *Destiny of the Daleks*, painting white is tough because it tends to bleach out easily with reproduction and especially with scanning. Those white Imperial Daleks are made up of quite a few layers of purple and pink, grey and even some blues. There's more to it than you would think. You think that a white Dalek is going to just be white. No, because it reflects all the colours that are around it.

Plus, there are the marble floors of Tranquil Repose. There's a bit of reflection with the Dalek close to the back of Colin Baker, so you can see little bands of white on the floor reproduced there. Daleks are difficult enough at the best of times, to get everything perfectly right, to make them look machine-like with very clean edges. To do that reversed, with darker colours on a lighter colour, is quite difficult: firstly, to draw and to space out; and then to paint; and to then cut those bronze-gold balls and have them all even and nicely spaced. That was very challenging.

This reference of Colin was a black-and-white still that I think had been sent as part of a promotional pack, and I had to colour it by hand. I haven't seen it much since, if ever. It must be one of those that just went AWOL, I guess. That costume is impactful, but colouring black-and-white versions was always a headache. Luckily, I'd already worked on Colin for the *Slipback* cover for *DWM*, and a few other earlier covers like *The Mark the Rani*. It was simply a case of remembering what you'd done before, and comparing other references to pop everything together and make it work.

The colours of the jacket are accentuated and blended downwards, into the surroundings of Tranquil Repose, where the crystal Dalek is. With that see-through Dalek, it was tricky to: a) find a good reference; and b) plot him out and paint him as though he's there but not there. You can see that the image was built over another Dalek base beneath. There are two sets of spheres to organise, and then the reflection through and off the mid sections – which gets muddled and confused even when you're looking at it, let alone reproducing the reference photo as well. And that's before you get up to the domed head over the decaying, augmented guy sat in the case.

Then I used a bit of the opening sequence effect behind. It was a good opportunity to get Terry Molloy's Great Healer head in as well. I wanted to get as much sculpted detail in there as I could, and have the light bounce reflections off the clear casing that surrounded him. It was a novel idea, having him in this almost TARDIS console-shaped case, like a cryogenically frozen head. Very *Futurama*.

(above) Original sketch for Revelation of the Daleks.
(opposite) Original VHS artwork.

REVELATION OF THE DALEKS (VHS)

TIMESLIDES: THE DOCTOR WHO ART OF COLIN HOWARD

TIME-FLIGHT (VHS)

Starring the Fifth Doctor, Tegan Jovanka, and Nyssa.
Never released. A version was released in July 2000 with a photographic collage cover by Black Sheep. *"That's not Hyde Park. It's Heathrow Airport."*

Unlike *Revelation of the Daleks*, I have no clue as to why *Time-Flight* was never used. Sad, really, as this was a neat chance to paint Concorde!

I've been on Concorde. Not to fly anywhere, I hasten to add. I'm not Joan Collins. I think it was at the Duxford Aviation Museum, relatively close to us in Norwich. They've got one of the Air France Concordes there. It's incredibly snug – if you're really tall, don't bother – with a very narrow fuselage. But it's an amazing aircraft; obviously, nothing else could get near it.

As a plane nut, I've painted a few aircraft in my time, and made God knows how many models. Here, I wanted to use Concorde to break things up and depict how it jumped through time. That splits up the cover, with the colour above going up to the usual space effect – although in this case, it's Earth's atmosphere. The cloud layer breaks things down further, showing this otherworldly destination. It's a nice way to gradate the core elements, getting in the textures of all the rocks and the intricate Aztec-like citadel.

Then I used Kalid's crystal ball to throw out light, similar to the technique I used for *The Five Doctors*' cover, with the Doctor blending in with that – a monochromatic effect, in a way, albeit a coloured version. You've got the nice contrast between that opaque, organic structure built over the sphere too, so that gives another point of interest. There's a painstaking building-up of layers, from mid-tone colours up to the white of the core of the energy spike from the crystal ball.

I've fond memories of the VHS range, but it goes alongside a real sadness. Going to Black Sheep was good for ensuring uniformity across the range, but there were so few other shows that had the idea to include original artwork for each story. The whole point of an artwork is that you have an original piece. If you do something on a computer, yes, you have the original file, but you wouldn't stick a microchip on the wall, would you? It gave us, as *Doctor Who* fans, something precious that, especially with Target covers, became groovier over time, and gained this status as the definite articles.

Black Sheep decided to junk that for homogeneity and Photoshop covers. And they made a killing doing that. In this day and age, there are computer programmes that can create a 'painting' people's likenesses, for example their profile photos on social media. It goes to show that people always like to see a picture of themselves, even if it's done by a machine.

Unless fans have childhood memories of owning the VHSes, I'm not sure loads of people will know my artwork, nor that of my peers from that era. We're the ones that have essentially been forgotten about, which is really sad when you consider the Target novels and how revered the artwork for those rightfully is.

It's strange that the last bastion of painted *Doctor Who* artwork, these VHS covers, has mostly been lost to time.

TIME-FLIGHT (VHS)

(opposite, left bottom) Original sketch for Time-Flight.
(below) Original VHS artwork.

TIMESLIDES: THE DOCTOR WHO ART OF COLIN HOWARD

BEAST OF FANG ROCK

Written by Andy Frankham-Allen. Published by Candy Jar Books in October 2015.
"There's always death on the rock when the Beast's about."

I was casting about a bit because I was planning to do some *Doctor Who* related art, and I thought, 'Where could I go?' And I had a message from Andy Frankham-Allen [*Lethbridge-Stewart* Range Editor] saying that they were thinking about doing this series of books about the Brigadier, and might I be interested in doing a cover? I like the Brigadier's character a lot, so I had a quick look at the format and said I'd be happy to take on a commission.

I was asked to do *Beast of Fang Rock*, which was good because I'm a sucker for Sontarans, so their mortal enemy was interesting to see: that strange vermicelli-ridden, glowing old thing in *Horror of Fang Rock* (1977). And Reuben was very chilling too.

With book covers, usually I'll work from a synopsis, where I'm told the kind of thing that's going to happen, plus any relevant visual descriptions. This was similar with my BBC Books work. You get a breakdown of what things might look like, or the descriptive text from the actual book, to then work out your sketch and try and to design something from that.

I wanted to go a bit wilder, with some Rutan tentacles coming off the actual circle, snaking up more towards the lighthouse, but I reined it in, to tie in with the rest of the books at that time. And Anne Travers is front and centre because I obviously recognised the character from *The Web of Fear*, and I think she had a fairly major part to play in the book.

Beast of Fang Rock had an afterword by Ralph Watson [who played Captain Ben Knight], and I went on to draw him a few times for the *Lethbridge-Stewart* series, including for *The Mind of Stone* (2016). The focal points are mostly characters from UNIT lore, so then you have to find reference material to work from, to actually use the portraits to represent them in the books. With *The Mind of Stone*, I probably took a Telesnap or screengrab from *The Web of Fear*, but then flipped it for the sake of the composition. That made the beret fold the wrong way, as was pointed out by some fans!

All my Candy Jar covers are painted with a graphics tablet and program, and around three hundred times magnification for intricate detail. I mess with pixels and paint at that resolution, so you end up with quite a realistic-looking painted version of, for instance, the moon in *Beast of Fang Rock*, rather than just photo manipulation.

That's how I worked in the agency years; I taught myself to do that kind of thing. You get a really nice, deeply toned, crisp image that will bear being blown up to a great degree. It's the equivalent of what I used to do traditionally, so it's just as time consuming.

When I started doing that kind of work, a friend gave me an old Compaq computer and a copy of Photoshop to play around with. I had that on loan from him for a few years, probably in the late 1990s. And then I just carried on from there in my spare time. One great advantage was that I was now able to work supplying digital artwork via email, or uploading directly to the publishers, cutting out the need for postage. And they could give me the pages to fit the artwork directly onto. It cut out the issue of anyone messing about with the artwork, because it was designed specifically to fit to their templates, rather than me having to work out the template only to have it not match, then having to crop it.

(above) Advert for the Lethbridge-Stewart *books, including my art for* Beast of Fang Rock *and* The Grandfather Infestation.
(opposite) Original novel artwork.

BEAST OF FANG ROCK

TIMESLIDES: THE DOCTOR WHO ART OF COLIN HOWARD

DOCTOR WHO MAGAZINE #167

Edited by John Freeman. Dated 28th November 1990.

This was a result of my constant submissions to John Freeman at *Doctor Who Magazine*, working on the archive stuff, and in the meantime trying to refine my painting and make it work better so that he might risk the huge danger of giving me a painted cover.

This was a fair while before the VHS covers. I went on to do a few more *Doctor Who Magazine* covers, and even *TVZone*, before I was finally given the opportunity to do the VHSes. It was a really lovely training ground for me. It made me a better painter.

This was actually painted on artboard, so it was a rigid, fairly thick piece of A2, a bit of a swine to scan in, to actually get the full artwork digitally. But I was just so excited to be doing an actual cover for *DWM*, a magazine I actually collected.

And then I see it in store and it's got an Abslom Daak flexidisc stuck over the front of it! Ah well. These things happen.

There was a nice Dalek claw hanging out of a ruined casing with some rubble at the bottom too, and that was totally wiped out by the banner about Graham Williams. It's great that now it's fully visible.

The other interesting thing was the big redesign of the Daleks for *Remembrance of the Daleks* (1988); up until then, you could safely rely on the fact that the Daleks hadn't really changed in quite some time. All of a sudden, we were presented with these white and gold versions, with different eye pieces and different flashing light mounts on their heads. It was quite a challenge to get hold of the reference material, especially with the reflective necks.

And the shuttlecraft that they designed and built a real-life model of – that was impressive; I immediately decided that we had to have that fully on the cover. It made a nice change that there was a bit of budget lavished on that one.

The worst aspect of getting assigned a Dalek story was 'Here we go, Daleks' balls again'. When you ever have to paint a Dalek, you're tearing out whatever hair you have left with the sheer amount of these spheres that you have to paint; you've got to get each one to

(above) Printed cover for DWM *#167.*

look pretty much alike the next; vary the angles of them; take perspective into account... It's an incredibly challenging beast to paint. But hey, *it's a Dalek*!

Despite this cover commission coming shortly after the unofficial cancellation of the series, the fandom, luckily, was still in healthy shape. In fact, at the time there seemed to be a big new swell of fans, a fair few conventions, and lots of independent fanzines. Clearly it was a big enough fanbase to keep interest in the show running. And a damn good job it was, isn't it?

I was really quite flattered when they did a poll for the Top 50 all-time *Doctor Who Magazine* covers. With over 54,500 total votes cast, this one made the list. That was really lovely, that it's still fondly remembered in that way.

DOCTOR WHO MAGAZINE #167

(below) Original artwork.

TIMESLIDES: THE DOCTOR WHO ART OF COLIN HOWARD

INVASION OF THE CAT-PEOPLE

Starring the Second Doctor, Ben Jackson, and Polly Wright. Written by Gary Russell. Released in August 1995.
"Explode the buoys? But that will destroy the Earth!"
"Oh dear, so it will. Pass on my apologies to the humans, won't you?"

I had a lot of fun with this one. It's one of my favourite covers I've done for *Doctor Who*-related stuff.

If you think of the idea of a cat walking upright, it's quite a ridiculous concept because of their physique. They're very long in the body and have these tiny little feet to stand and sit on… and I had then to put that form into a skin-tight red leather catsuit – and *then* have them with weapons! They have no opposable thumbs, so holding a weapon would be incredibly difficult. I had to think sort of laterally… What on earth would this weapon look like, and how might they hold them?

The main three cats on the cover are Gary Russell's and mine. Tarot and Scratch were both Gary's cats, and then one of ours, the black one with the white bib, was Albert. He was mine and Michelle's first cat, who we got about a month before we married in 1992.

We had Albert for a very long time, and he helped raise a few others from kittens because he was such a lovely, gentle cat. He was very nurturing, which was quite weird for a little boy. I love cats. We had Twiglet from the RSPCA, then Charlie, who was a grey-and-white little cat. We think he was abducted from our local pub because he used to wander over the road and be fussed over there. One night, he disappeared and we never saw him again. Afterwards, we had a brother and sister, Poppy and Murphy: she was a little tortoiseshell and Murphy was a big silly ginger puss, who lasted until he was about twenty. We had another ginger cat, George, who we got as a companion for Murphy after we lost Poppy, and he lived to a good age too. He was late teens; he was an RSPCA cat so his date of birth was unknown.

We've now got another brother and sister, part Maine Coon, one with the most massive tail, like a big feather duster. He's named after Ziggy Stardust, and she's Suki. She's sleek and black – more like Sutekh the Destroyer, because she's absolutely mental. She runs around the place like a mad thing. In fact, currently she's screaming to be let outside.

I'm happy that Albert lives on in this cover artwork.

Invasion of the Cat-People is all on one piece of card, with a lot of masking tape used. The *Missing Adventures* have a specific formula: you have the title box at the top right and then the author, etc., bottom right. You're given a column on the left where you have the Doctor and companion(s), and the descriptive narrative illustration in the middle on the right.

It's painted from black-and-white references, so Patrick Troughton is from *Fury from the Deep* – sans bobble hat! – and I think Ben and Polly are from publicity shots, but I popped them together like that and researched colours particularly for her costume. It was a chance for me to show what I could do with portraits, and even with black-and-white material, so they could take me a little more seriously as an artist for cover work (it didn't quite work out that way).

Of course, then there's the landing craft. That was something I designed. I tried to evoke the idea of cats' eyes on the front of the pointed attack ship. The description said that it should be highly reflective, so that it would become almost invisible when flying. That was a nice idea, having this stark contrast between the red earth of the Australian outback and the blue sky.

INVASION OF THE CAT-PEOPLE

(opposite left) Pencils for Invasion of the Cat-People.
(below) Original artwork.

TIMESLIDES: THE DOCTOR WHO ART OF COLIN HOWARD

VIRGIN DECALOG

Lost Property published on 20th July 1995.

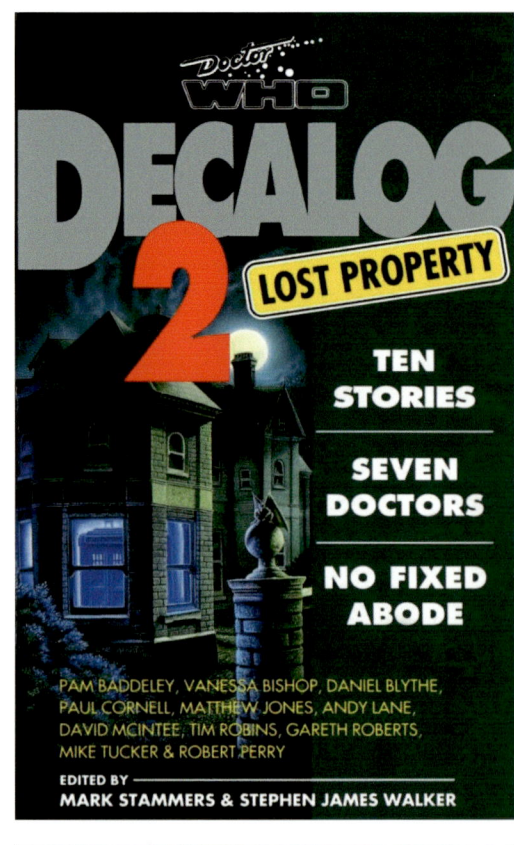

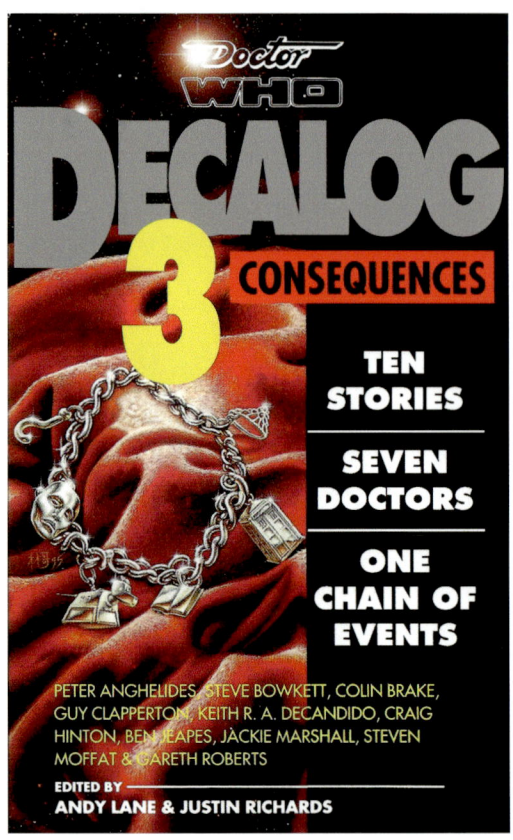

VIRGIN DECALOG: LOST PROPERTY & CONSEQUENCES

Consequences published on 18th July 1996.

My background with agency work came in handy again here. I had to follow a creative brief and design things that would fit with the stories. Sometimes you're given a short descriptive passage, or the author will give you some notes as to how things should look. You'll then come up with a visualisation of that brief. It's something you have to do a lot in agency work: following set, strict guidance, keeping within those parameters.

The brief for *Lost Property* was to do a townhouse with the TARDIS inside it. So I went wandering around the neighbourhood, and the one you see on the cover was actually a house up Lower Clarence Road, adjacent to where we lived in Norwich. I headed home and drew it from memory, then made up little bits and pieces. It was a case of having fun with the gloomy foreboding exterior and then the TARDIS' blue light illuminating the front room where it's materialised.

Then, with the gateway, we've got a little flying beastie on the sphere – a sort of cross between Bok from *The Dæmons* and a Mandrake from *The Golden Voyage Of Sinbad* (1973) with Tom Baker.

I was just given a brief piece of text with their idea for what might work to link the stories. And for *Consequences*, for some reason, it was a charm bracelet.

I can't remember whether I was instructed precisely what the charms should be, but I was very finicky with the detail. Especially with K9: you can really zoom in on him and see the ridiculous levels that I went to. The original artwork is only A4, but it's heavy on the detail. Also, if you look at the felt that the bracelet's sat on, you can see a lot of the individual fibres that I've painted and played with.

(opposite middle) The printed covers for Virgin Decalog *books 2 and 3.*
(right and opposite left) Actual artwork.

TIMESLIDES: THE DOCTOR WHO ART OF COLIN HOWARD

THE MASQUE OF MANDRAGORA COMIC

From a script by Louis Marks; colours by Steve Whitaker; lettering by Sophie Heath. Printed in *Doctor Who Magazine* #161 (1990). Edited by John Freeman.

Back in the late 1980s, I was going to every *Doctor Who* event I could, taking along my little black-and-white portfolio, or if I felt particularly lucky, some prints to sell. I showed John Freeman my work and asked if there was any possibility of some work at *Doctor Who Magazine*.

He seemed interested in assigning me comic strips and thought the *DWM* Archive series might be a good starting point. I was very happy because the first one was *The Masque of Mandragora*, featuring Sarah Jane and Tom's Doctor. That was a lovely chance to get. I rewatched the start of part one on a home-recorded VHS, then tried to condense it down into an opening strip. I thought it would be an interesting idea to incorporate a vortex swirl into the lower half of the artwork. This would meld together and draw you into the TARDIS as the Mandragora Helix hitched a ride.

My first exposure to comics was probably American imports given to me by one of my uncles. These were the A5 colour versions that would fold out. Spider-Man was the first one. I especially loved the Green Goblin. I do remember the first one I bought myself, *The Night Gwen Stacy Died* [*The Amazing Spider-Man* #121–122 (1973)]. This featured her demise at the hideous hands of the Goblin. I absolutely loved all that.

It was escapism and fed my love for all things graphic and weird. I felt a particular fondness for the more monstrous antagonists, like the Lizard, and villains who dabbled in mentality and delusion, like Mysterio. I started to draw some of the pages to keep myself entertained. As a young, artistically minded individual, I assimilated these things and wanted to emulate them.

I was always drawing animals and things like that, but with exposure to sci-fi movies, I was pushed towards comics and fantasy books. Those set off an artistic fire within me.

Starting out, I worked for a few fanzines like *Cosmic Masque* and *Cloister Bell*. I would do *Doctor Who* comic strips, but I wasn't really a writer; my strips were always more focused on the sensational look of things. Later on, I did a British comic called *Space Junk*. Nicholas Briggs asked me to draw this *Quatermass*-inspired character, Leon Barnabas OBE. I worked on that for about nine issues, or however long it ran.

I think the problem with comics for me was my interest in doing detail. I would have to spend way too long on each page, putting too much into it. This was the problem with *The Masque of Mandragora*: I used way too much black and did not leave enough for the colourist to do. I coloured the next one, *Terror of the Autons*, myself to save annoying anybody!

John obviously saw I was keen on detail and that my likenesses, for the most part, weren't too bad. That's probably why he asked if I'd help with the *DWM* Archive. It was either keep using the same old reference photos over and over, or come up with something new, so I spent a while doing these intricate black-and-white Frank Bellamy and Chris Achilléos -inspired dot work illustrations.

(left) The final coloured comic, as printed in DWM #161.
(opposite) Original artwork.

THE MASQUE OF MANDRAGORA COMIC

TIMESLIDES: THE DOCTOR WHO ART OF COLIN HOWARD

DOCTOR WHO MAGAZINE #192

Dated 28th October 1992. Edited by Gary Russell.

It was my idea to give the original art for this cover away. I thought this would help raise my profile. Sadly, at the time, I was being assassinated by some fanzines. I thought that I needed to try and get a few more people on my side.

So how could I attempt to do this? I hid about seventeen names and initials in the Chief Sea Devil and surroundings. *DWM* then reported, 'If you can find them all, someone at *DWM* will pick a name out of a hat and the lucky winner will get the original artwork.' It was a lot of work, but ultimately worth it.

The great thing about that particular issue was that I painted it on A3, and then the poster they gave away was A2. It doubled the size of everything I'd written in the artwork, making it so much easier for people to find the hidden text. Nonetheless, I planned it out so that nothing would be hidden by the barcode, cover logo, etc…

If you want to play the game yourself, the full answers are upside-down on this page!

I based this one on the Chief Sea Devil, with the slightly different design to incorporate his working mouth. This was mightily impressive in the original serial. I was trying to tie elements from the show into one image. There's the scanner where the Sea Devils are watching the navy vessels looming towards them, and the submarine on its mission to try and find the underwater base. But I also wanted to incorporate some more reality, hence all the weed fronds growing up from the seabed, and the odd little fish in there as well. Why make things easy when you can torture yourself with ridiculous levels of detail!?

But it's lovely when it all comes off. All the bubbles going up from the seabed towards the submarine tie things together, with everything running into its adjacent partner; even the cliff wall fades up into the Earth, where the base is located.

Answers: Some are obvious: Jon Pertwee, Roger Delgado; my wife, Michelle too. And they're mostly friends: 'PW' is Pete Wallbank; 'GR' is Gary Russell; and 'JF' is John Freeman. Dale is one of my good friends in Norwich, as is Eamonn. John and Heather are cousins, and Sam was their little boy, who was also a *Doctor Who* fan at the time. 'Paul B' and 'Paul V' are close to each other: they're Paul Barrett and Paul Vasquez. Vickie and Derek are local friends of mine from a long time ago.

Tim was the first *Doctor Who* fan I met who lived in the area. I met him at DWASocial 5 (1985) at the Novotel in Hammersmith, London, and by the time we got back to Norwich, I was stranded, and he drove me back 20 miles from Norwich to Harleston, and then he went off back home to Lowestoft. And that was the beginning of a long friendship, as we're still in touch to this day. Plus, the final 17th name? My signature! That was an easy one…

(above right) The printed cover.
(opposite) DWM *poster.*

DOCTOR WHO MAGAZINE #192

TIMESLIDES: THE DOCTOR WHO ART OF COLIN HOWARD

DOCTOR WHO CLASSIC COMICS #11

Dated 15th September 1993. Edited by Gary Russell.
Reprinting *The Doctor Strikes Back* (*TV Comic* #792-795), and Part Two of *The Tides of Time* (*Doctor Who Monthly* #65-68).

Big thanks to John Freeman for sticking with me on the *DWM* Archive. I continued to send him copies of my paintings as I improved. I did the cover for *TV Zone* #30 in 1992, when *The Tomb of the Cybermen* was recovered [officially in 1991] and released on VHS. That was a nice piece of design: it was an A3 painting with that iconic Cyberman erupting from its cell, the Cyber-Controller at the bottom, and the Cybermats at the base. By that time, I had pretty much cracked it when it came to technique.

(above) Original pencils for Classic Comics *#11.*
(opposite) Original artwork.

Then John started to ask me to do covers for *DWM*, and when he moved on from the magazine, Gary Russell took over and carried on using me, which was lovely of him. And this led to covers for *Doctor Who Classic Comics*, the reprints of the old '60s and some '70s comic strips, which Gary also edited for its three-year run.

The *Classic Comics* were great to do, but had a very awkward layout. The titles came down quite a way, there was this beast of a barcode at the bottom, and often text going across. They always had this column on the left hand side. This would drop down and would often curtail your artwork. So this one's a bit abstract, quite simply to do something a bit different with it.

For #11, however, that played in nicely, because I could achieve this almost mirror-parallel of the column to the left. I wanted to play around with the geometric shapes that were banging around at the time, and cutting down through the top of the Dalek was, I thought, a great way to get Patrick Troughton on the cover without using the usual floating head or bust that would fade into the background.

There is a hint of the creature inside the Dalek from the shadowplay on its skirt section, plus a tease of something *other* around the back of the neck – although the latter is essentially the start of Pat's paisley hanky, merging into the Dalek mesh. It's good to keep these things obscure where you can, so they're open to interpretation.

The reference for the Doctor is a moody shot from *The Three Doctors* – lots of dark shapes which work quite nicely with the Dalek city structure to the right (from a studio reference photo) and the vivid red, cracking circle to the left – again basically mirroring each other on either side of Troughton. If you've got a dark figure, it pops out more if you place it against something light – in this case, the silver Dalek standing out against the blackness of the Doctor's frame. And then I added in some crackling effect, just to keep myself happy.

If you get up close you can spot little details such as the Doctor's clip-on bow tie. If you can achieve a level of detail where you can see light playing off the head of a pin or whatever, that's fun to do. It's a good learning process. Quite honestly, it's nice to look back and see my progression to this stage. I was getting more competent and was now able to pull off such things.

DOCTOR WHO CLASSIC COMICS #11

TIMESLIDES: THE DOCTOR WHO ART OF COLIN HOWARD

CLASSIC COMICS AUTUMN HOLIDAY

Dated 1993. Edited by Gary Russell.
Reprinting *Evening's Empire* from *Doctor Who Magazine* #180 (1991).

This is a very good demonstration of just how much space was available on the covers of *Classic Comics*. You can see how far across that column went, how far the title would come down – that's the sort of thing that you live with as a commercial artist: you are aware of the area that you have to work in and you stick to those guidelines. That was the strange thing with the BBC, specifically the VHS range; everything was laid out to be precise, yet the reproduction company, for some reason, was so varied when applying the design. They got the covers delivered to them with everything already laid out, and all they had to do was scan the whole thing.

This painting is A2, which is a large surface area to work on. Most of the *Classic Comics* pieces were massive because, at the time, editorial seemed very aware that, with some artists, you didn't know how rough their work was going to be. The bigger it was, the more it could be reduced, and the better it would look. To some degree, I was a victim of this, as it made everything take slightly longer. But, as I continued doing them, it became obvious that I could work smaller while retaining just as much detail. That's how I managed to persuade them to go down to A3. Otherwise, it was a lot to mask off, to paint, to airbrush, to get the whole concept down. I find it easier to work on a smaller scale – around A3 is my comfort zone. This change also made it easier to meet their tight turnaround times. I think I usually had about a week from being told what was required, to actually having to produce the artwork.

I'm happy with this piece. It was strange how it came about, though. It was written by Andrew Cartmel, edited by John Freeman, and drawn by Richard Piers Rayner, whose art is so clean and beautiful; a fantastic standard to achieve. It was an honour doing the cover for this strip. Still, only the first part of *Evening's Empire* was published in *Doctor Who Magazine* itself. The story suffered behind-the-scenes delays, so it wasn't until 1993 that it was completed. The *Doctor Who Classic Comics Autumn Holiday Special*, therefore, was the first time it was published in full.

There are some nice portraits here, like Sophie from *Survival*. I envisioned the main character for the strip as… well, basically Madonna! I took a frame out of the comic strip, fleshed it out, and gave it my version of 3D realism, hence the wetsuit and the breathing apparatus. Again, a lot of detail on Sylvester, but at least I found a picture without the handkerchief tied around his hat, which would've required even more precise detailing…

Moving down, the Doctor's jumper merges with the deceased airman with his Messerschmitt Bf 109 that crashed into the canal (or whatever it was – it sure was a while ago). Poor chap obviously lost his front teeth in the crash – maybe face-planting the joystick, who knows? It's good to play around with something broodier than your standard promo shots on the cover.

The background makes this pop, but it's not one-tone. I airbrushed in different oranges, etc., because otherwise, it's a bit dull solely to have this slab of colour. That's why I had the marble effect on that background panel too, mixing black and green. "Red and green should never be seen", eh?

(above) The printed cover for the Autumn Holiday Special.
(opposite) *Original artwork.*

THE ELEVEN DOCTORS

TIMESLIDES: THE DOCTOR WHO ART OF COLIN HOWARD

FACE THE RAVEN

Starring the Twelfth Doctor and Clara Oswald | 2016.
"What's the point of being a doctor if I can't cure you?"

This was one of the stories from that era that I really took to. Around that time, I was doing quite a few private commissions featuring Clara Oswald and Amy Pond for one particular guy, and I hoped he'd ask for my take on *Face the Raven*. I pitched the idea to him, but unfortunately, just the week before, he'd commissioned another artist to do this episode! I figured, "I'll do it anyway," and I'm glad I did, because I ended up keeping the original.

It channels my love of classic illustration, where you'd have this background with a cut-out symbolic shape, which here further reflects the Gallifreyan script. The Gallifreyan is mostly lifted directly from the show, and then it's just a lot of painstaking compass work. Getting the ratios correct for all those concentric circles was challenging; I think there are quite a few compass holes at the centres of the circles. That was with a propelling pencil, which I prefer to your standard HB as it allows you to be more precise. This being A3, I think I used a pair of compasses at full stretch to achieve the largest circle.

Again, I start at the back and move forwards, even in individual sections of the painting. You can see how jet-black the Raven initially was, then from that base colour, I worked up with little variations in shading and colours – purples, blues, browns, greens, almost up to pure titanium white for the light high points. The same for Clara and the Doctor: I'm slowly, piece by piece, building up many layers of paint, until you get to the lightest pinks and ivories, yellows and whites.

The gorgeous old cobbles of Trap Street, surrounded by beamed buildings, felt like a decent change from the sci-fi related imagery I'm mostly associated with. Being a bit of a twitcher, I enjoyed doing the close-up of the Raven having a good old squawk. Plus, this is the end for Clara, wearing that stunning costume with the intricate lace, and in that pose, echoing the crucifixion. It was a particularly punchy picture.

The Raven essentially doing that same pose worked nicely, but it took a lot of freeze-framing to get the positioning just right. The other option was a side profile of the Raven and Clara, but that would've worked better if it were the other way around, i.e. an *Alien* sort of thing, with the Raven bursting *out* – but this was impactful, going into Clara.

That's how I got that expression on the Doctor's face too, through pausing a recording. I definitely wanted to do a traditional portrait of Peter Capaldi; up to that point, I hadn't really tackled his Doctor before, except for in one digital piece. There's still a steely look, yes, but also a sad resignation. This is taken from when he follows Clara and watches her sacrifice. You can see a warmth in his eyes that was relatively rare from his Doctor then. That was important to get across: rather than this somewhat harsh, Hartnell-esque visage, he'd have these heartening tender moments that would often be overlooked.

(left) A progress picture for Face the Raven.
(opposite) Original artwork.
(overleaf) Progress photos for Scream of the Shalka.

FACE THE RAVEN

TIMESLIDES: THE DOCTOR WHO ART OF COLIN HOWARD

SCREAM OF THE SHALKA

Starring an alternative Ninth Doctor and Alison Cheney | 2021.

A nice chap in America asked if I'd do a *Scream of the Shalka* commission, and I'd never actually watched it. The story came at a bad time for me: I'd basically been let go from the *Doctor Who* covers, so I'd gone elsewhere looking for work. Everything was a bit raw, especially as *Shalka* is the type of project I would've loved to have been involved with. When I was commissioned, I sat down to watch it and they did a great job. So then I suggested that, instead of doing it animation style, I did a classic realistic painted version of the characters.

I've always liked Richard E Grant – I was a big fan of *Withnail and I* (1987) – and this reference shot, I believe, came from *Star Wars: The Rise of Skywalker* (2019). I slotted him into the *Shalka* outfit (and added on that extreme hairdo), as I did with Sophie Okonedo as Alison. I liked the Master as a droid, so opted to remove part of Derek Jacobi's face (not something you often say) without the flap hanging over his ear, and then factored in that amazing TARDIS set!

I painted this all by hand because I'd previously dropped my airbrush, thanks to my MS. It landed needle-point first on a wooden floor. Split the nozzle. The fine spray now gives off an odd, jagged pattern. It's a beautiful airbrush, a Canopus design (rebranded as a single action Rotring Modelle E), which I bought in the '90s for the VHSes; I'd sourced replacement parts from Germany. I've still got my original compressor I bought with it too.

My work rate is much slower now, so this easily took two months, maybe more. A more recent composition took four and a half months. Still, being able to continue painting, even as a hobby, is a great release of creativity for me.

  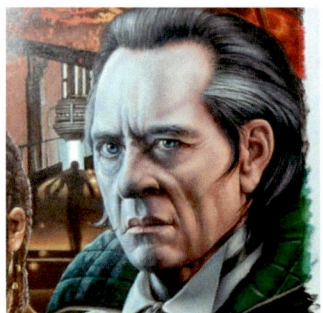 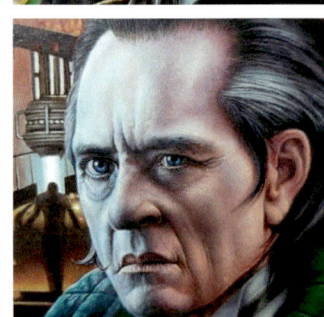

SCREAM OF THE SHALKA

TIMESLIDES: THE DOCTOR WHO ART OF COLIN HOWARD

ANIMATIONS

Charles Norton interviewed me back in the day for *DWM*, and he very kindly remembered me when he became producer on the *Doctor Who* animations. He asked me if I'd return to do a cover for *The Power of the Daleks*. No offence, but that's a silly question! *Of course I would!*

I was put in touch with another person who asked for some rough ideas (and even sent some movie posters that he suggested I might do *Doctor Who* versions of); Charles seemed appalled that I'd been asked to supply these six or so images as an idea of what I might do on the cover. And after all that, they didn't seem to like any of them. I ended up having to do something with Daleks, then was asked to add the Doctor, Ben, and Polly. But I couldn't flesh them out using photographic references because it was deemed misrepresentative of the content. Everything was based on the character animation designs by Martin Geraghty.

I then produced this entirely black-and-white image, painted traditionally from Titanium White through to Mars Black. That was my pallet allocation – no colour because *Power of the Daleks* was going to be black-and-white. And then BBC America insisted that a colour version was included…

I digitally added some blue to the Dalek spheres, to the energy weapons, touches here and there to give an idea of what was featured in the animation. As the animations went on, the covers essentially became versions of what I did on *Power*, with the monsters in front and the TARDIS team above. Sadly, that was my first and last animation cover.

Then I had another nice surprise: after delivering the artwork, Charles contacted me again and said, "We've just realised we don't have a TARDIS exterior for materialisation and dematerialisation shots in episodes one and six. Could you supply a TARDIS?" Being asked to help producing the show that I absolutely adored, why would I say no?

So I sent in a massively detailed TARDIS exterior I'd digitally painted, essentially to prove I could be relied upon for this sort of thing – I did the TARDIS on a weekend, and it was ready for them on the Monday morning. Rather unfortunately, I was erased in the special edition of *Power*, with my TARDIS swapped for one they'd used in *The Faceless Ones* (I guess for continuity).

Nonetheless, they asked if I would consider doing background elements for more. The first texture wraps I did were used in *Shada*, but I also provided flat sets for that, to be wrapped onto things like floors, walls, and computer terminals. And I did the TARDIS monitor!

ANIMATIONS

Working on the animations can be quite time consuming, and now and again, I get to be artistic, although not that often with the animations. The tapestry is a nice example. It was for the stairwell fight between Jamie and Kemel in *The Evil of the Daleks*. Maxtible's house was actually Grim's Dyke Mansion House in Middlesex. There were some good quality screengrabs from another production that was shot there in the late '60, early '70s, so I was able to look at those four or five different photos and work out what was on the real-life tapestry. I managed to lift some of the colours from those pictures too.

Of course, you've then got to make sure it looks stitched, not painted, which is why there's very muted, pale tones in the landscape background, getting brighter and bolder as you come forwards. The closer you get to the viewpoint, the darker it gets, and you can show off a bit more detail. You get sort of lost in the piece and feel as though you can travel into that painting. I think the border was based on the actual tapestry as well, which is still hanging in that manor house, as far as I'm aware.

Accuracy is always paramount, certainly with *Doctor Who*, because you're trying to give as faithful a version of the original show as possible. We were given access to the set designs, production drawings, photographs taken on set at the time of filming, and you use all of these to check through the various parts of what you're working on. For *The Macra Terror*, we had a good set of black-and-white photos, even apart from telesnaps – some taken by the production team at the time, whether it's the set designer or someone who built it, wanting a record of what they've achieved. On all the ones I worked on, we had incredibly detailed replicas of what actually went on screen.

The Evil of the Daleks took about sixteen months, on and off, and I didn't really have time to work on anything else during that time. This was my first time working with [animation director and producer] AnneMarie Walsh too – before that, I had been working with Charles Norton [who took on those roles for the *Shada* and *The Power of the Daleks* animations]. This was a different way of working. Things have changed with how the BBC do these things; for instance, it's an hourly or daily rate now, rather than just me being given a list of illustrations to provide for backgrounds. Certainly for *The Macra Terror*, I was working alongside Graham Bleathman, and they would divide up the background requirements between us, so we'd get a list of settings and images that were needed.

It's fun, working with other artists, even indirectly. There's the portrait of Deborah Watling in *Evil*: I was presented with the animated character art by Martin Geraghty. That had the pose they needed, because the animation was going to fade through from the actual portrait, through to Victoria in the cell. I used Martin's drawing as a background template, then fleshed out the 2D look, giving it the depth and texture a painting might have on the wall. But that caused other issues. I didn't think about changing the dress colour or anything like that. I think they ended up just tinting it all purple for the painting to segue through to the colours used on Victoria's dress in the animation, to differentiate her from her mother (despite the pair looking identical).

Strict daily guidance can be tough when you factor in my MS. In the past, you would simply supply an image to be used used as a backdrop; now, you're wrapping texture surfaces onto 3D objects, so you're limited by the shapes that you're given. It's not quite as creative as you'd

(left) The portrait of Victoria Waterfield, based on the character design (far left) by Martin Geraghty. (below) The printed DVD cover for The Power of the Daleks *animation.*

TIMESLIDES: THE DOCTOR WHO ART OF COLIN HOWARD

like. It involves far more head scratching as you work out angles, especially if you're supplied with a model that isn't straight on, or at the right angles to match things up.

You have to do it all by eye. Take the house from *The Evil of the Daleks* for instance. That wasn't presented as a straight shot, and it was *a lot* of bricks – and they all have to match up. If it's not a straight shot, it's no longer an easy perspective to draw things from. It's quite a challenge to make everything look right; it's incredibly involved, complicated work.

Gavin Rymill made a model of the manor, produced at a specific angle; it's that aerial shot in *Evil*. The traditional method is front-on, so you'd have a front elevation, left, right, top, etc., and then use a textual wrap to fold around it, like origami. But because this was such an intricate building, they decided to just go for one angle, and asked me to wrap it from that perspective. But buildings are mostly made up of verticals, right angles, horizontal lines, and so on, so when viewed at an angle, it mostly doesn't have these lines in the correct places.

Essentially, I had to approximate everything, to transform and distort the imagery so that the lines would fit for perspective's sake. No right angle would remain the same. That was the biggest challenge that I had. I think it was about five or six sections of the manor house I had to wrap, and each section took me about three days, possibly longer, to do. Even my new computer struggled with it! If I printed off the actual artwork for that house, it would be about three and a half metres long.

One thing was a great help: the production team went on a day trip to the house and took reams of photographs. The model used on screen is pretty faithful to the actual house.

I taught myself to do it. I analyse things and work out what would go well together as a composition (that's true of paintings and textures like this) and how to present things. If you've got a creative mind, it doesn't really matter if you've been formally trained or not.

(below) The finished tapestry, as seen in The Evil of the Daleks *animation.*
(opposite) Three stages of Maxtible's mansion in The Evil of the Daleks. *From top: the full front-view wrap; applying textures; and side-view of the manor.*

106

ANIMATIONS

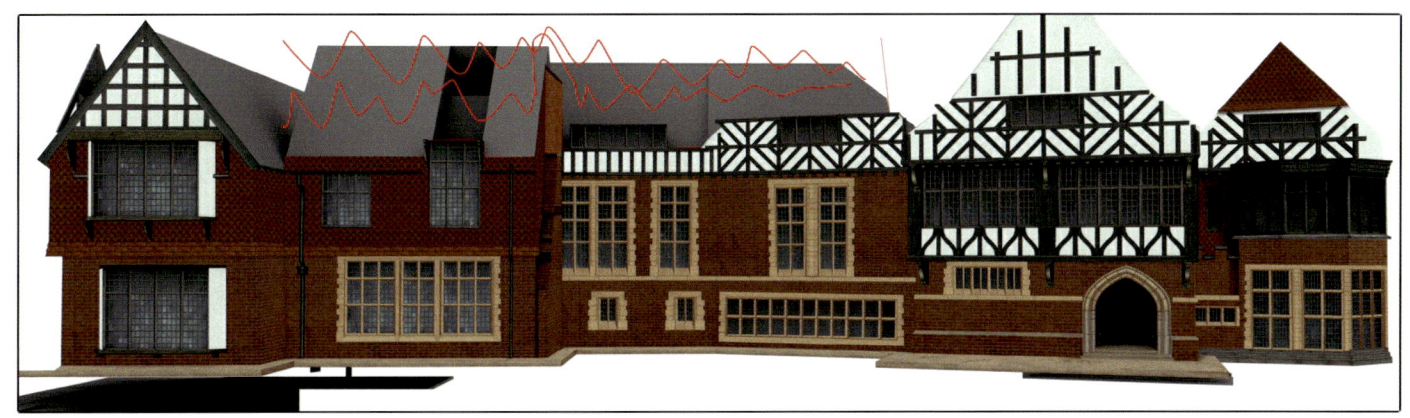

TIMESLIDES: THE DOCTOR WHO ART OF COLIN HOWARD

THE MACRA TERROR

Starring the Second Doctor, Ben Jackson, and Polly Wright | 2019.
"There's no such thing as Macra."

I thought a nice thing for me to do, especially with my history doing VHS covers, would be to produce a piece of artwork to celebrate working on the animations. I figured, "Great, this is what I'm doing now. These animations will be ongoing." I thought I'd produce a cover for *The Macra Terror*, in the style of the VHSes. They were doing the BFI events, so I would take A4 prints along and give them to the people who worked on my team. It was a bit of a laugh, yes, but also a homage, and, admittedly, something to show what I could still be doing, if given the chance.

(And any excuse to do the Macra! They should've looked very disturbing, actually threatening and mobile, with these massive, gaping claws!)

Unfortunately, a lot of the team weren't there on the day. I waited around at the BFI bar, hoping to chat to some friendly faces, but there were very few to be seen. Unbeknownst to me, things had changed behind the scenes, and this "cover" turned out to be a farewell gift. That's the life of a self-employed freelancer: without knowing it, you can be surplus to requirements. A great shame. The team was being pared right down, and the first thing to go was us background artists.

There was nothing for a little while, then I heard from Rob Ritchie. He told me that *The Evil of the Daleks* was happening, and asked if I could help him out because he was getting snowed under. They required a lot of backgrounds they didn't have in stock. Whereas they can reuse stuff like concrete walls, *Evil* had too many intricate bits to do. In a way, it was nice, because I enjoyed working with Rob (and I hope vice versa), and I'd provided digital wraps before, on *Shada* for instance.

At Charles Norton's insistence, my work was done traditionally on *The Macra Terror*. He wanted things to have a hand-painted grain, not simply flat, shiny digital work. We had a massive heat wave at the time, so I was having issues with all my paints drying out much sooner than I wanted them to!

I shot myself in the foot, too, by putting graffiti carved in the walls of Medok's cell. As an inmate, you sit there for however long, you're a bit bored (I'm not gleaning from personal experience, I should add!)... so I added little messages either Medok or previous prisoners had carved into the rock. "Medok was right"; "Don't trust the Controller"; "The Macra exist" – that kind of stuff. I put some friends' names in there too. Then Charles told me he wanted additional angles of the cell, so I had to repaint everything in position

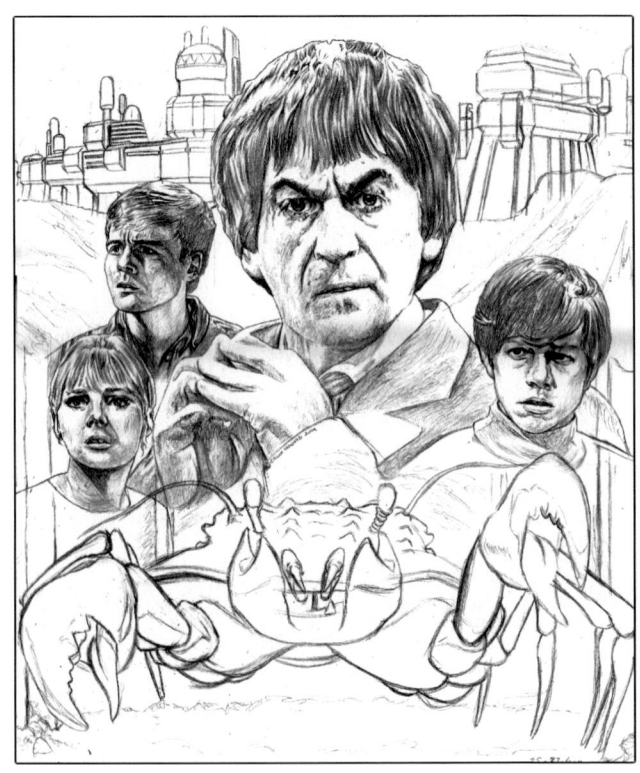

(above) Original pencils for The Macra Terror.
(opposite) Original artwork.

from different POVs. For that graffiti, I worked out what positions near the bench they were, at what heights, how many bricks high and how far along…

Rob added the bars afterwards, and it was lovely seeing the result. That's why I do them. It's not for the pay. To see your work on screen and your name in the titles is phenomenal. It's a sense of achievement: the same way that lifting up *Attack of the Cybermen* and seeing my name on that, having painted the cover, was. Or lifting up the VHSes and seeing "Cover Illustration by Colin Howard". That's what motivated me and made me think I might just have achieved something in my life. That's all you really want, to leave a mark. It's also the fact that I could help Charles, Rob, the team, and I did as good a job as I could, regardless of time constraints.

When all's said and done, it's the show I love. That's why this book exists too.

THE MACRA TERROR

TIMESLIDES: THE DOCTOR WHO ART OF COLIN HOWARD

TIMEWAVE: THE RIPPLES MADE BY COLIN'S ART

You've seen Colin's artistic journey, but any creative enterprise is a tapestry of stories. A painting, a sketch, a text, a book: all are made up of these intricate layers. The creator of this art and those who experience it: each bring their own contexts to the piece. There's an old adage about where true beauty lies. Here is a small selection of the beholders.

ROB SHEARMAN
Screenwriter, *Dalek*.

The Daleks *illustration (1987)*.

We're fast approaching the sixtieth anniversary, and I suppose that's quite exciting. But it's nothing to the fervour of nearing the *twentieth* back when you're thirteen years old, and you know that *Doctor Who* is the most important thing in the entire world. I hadn't been a fan long; having been terrified of Tom Baker's face and those scary time tunnel opening credits, it took Peter Davison and that impending anniversary to lead me in.

And the best way a thirteen-year-old could show his passion for something was to start a fanzine about it. Back in the days before Twitter, if you wanted to moan to the world about the quality of the Sea Devils in *Warriors of the Deep*, you had to do it the hard way: writing long articles, publishing them as photocopied stapelled zines, and flogging them at conventions.

My school had two fanzines: *Time Key* was edited by David Williams, before he tweaked his name and went on to create *Little Britain*. I was part of *Cloister Bell*, founded by an older boy named Owen Bywater. I was invited to write little pieces about the latest episodes and Target novelisations, and we went into London a few times to interview stars of the show with our little tape recorder. Over the next few years, thanks to diligence, obsessive dedication, and the fact my dad owned a printing firm and could make our magazine look halfway decent, I rose through the ranks from deputy editor to assistant editor to co-editor.

The truth is – *Cloister Bell* was awful. We had nothing to say. We'd complain about what we loved, because that's how you proved your love was real. We had a regular feature called the *Doctor Who Encyclopaedia*, in which we'd write reviews of every single story in order, in spite of the fact we'd never seen them and in most cases could only guess what their plots were from single paragraph synopses in the *Doctor Who Programme Guide*.

By rights, we should have been chased out of the Appreciation Society. But we had a secret weapon.

I'm not quite sure when Colin Howard wrote to us – and I certainly can't even begin to fathom *why*. But he'd read our fanzine and asked whether we would like some free artwork to accompany our articles. He sent us a multi-page comic story which detailed the adventures of Nyssa after she'd left the series. It was strangely brilliant. It was set on Terminus and featured the Cybermen, and somehow managed to combine the grimy atmosphere of the one and the exciting action of the other. As a humourless fan with very dismissive ideas about fan fiction and canon, I remember feeling guilty by just how much I was blown away by Colin's work. It was quite obviously the best thing in the fanzine – it had energy and humour – it wasn't just passive reaction to a television show, it was properly *creative* – both inspired by something Colin loved, and therefore too genuinely inspiring.

We kept the magazine going for a few more years – only losing its way during the depressing hiatus, and because Owen was preparing to study at Oxford. But from that point on, every single issue we released was dominated by the art of Colin Howard. No need to read what I thought about *Fury From the Deep* – Colin's portmanteau representation of it was stunning. Each issue, we would tell him what articles we were writing, and he'd gamely provide the artwork to sit beside it. It should have been the other way round.

And I remember how proud we were when Colin became a professional, and went on to produce covers for Target. That one of us had got to work on *Doctor Who*.

I ended up as a writer, some years later. I don't think it was *Cloister Bell* that got me there. My work on it was unrelentingly awful. But I do know that it was the unexpected success of the magazine that encouraged me to keep writing – and that success was because Colin raised our profile and made us try harder. Looking back, I do think Colin Howard showed me what the building blocks to a job in the arts really are: passion, dedication, real skill, and trying to make everyone else around you look better.

GARY RUSSELL
Former Editor, *Doctor Who Magazine, Doctor Who Classic Comics.*

I honestly don't know when I first met Colin face to face. I mean I know when I first became aware of his awesome talent as an artist – John Freeman, then editor of *Doctor Who Magazine*, showed me his painted cover for an issue based around *Remembrance of the Daleks*. I recall being suitably dismayed that most of the art was going to be hidden beneath a stupid flexidisc cover-mount and thinking, *Oh, stick the silly flexidisc on the back*. Probably not the first mad thought I ever had about cover-mounts and certainly not the last.

Colin's dynamic art for that cover was great. Painted covers for *DWM* were still very much a rarity and it was nice to see one so bright and, well, summery!

A few years later, I suspect I met Colin at a *DWM* signing at Café Munchen. By then, I had edged my way into Marvel UK and took over John's job, not only overseeing *DWM* but launching its sister title, *Doctor Who Classic Comics*, in 1992. Both magazines gave me the opportunity, whenever the budget allowed, to feature far more painted covers than ever before. *Classic Comics* especially so. I made it my mission to use Colin more than any other artist on *Classic Comics* – so poor Colin not only had to draw endless Dalek covers but also got to do Kleptons, Frobisher, and Beep the Meep – such was the diversity of characters created for the comic strips over the years. And every time, he jumped at the opportunity with enthusiasm and a clarity of vision that I liked. 'Think Kleptons' or 'Look again at *Stars Fell on Stockbridge*' or 'It's that Sixth Doctor story with the half-human/half-

TIMESLIDES: THE DOCTOR WHO ART OF COLIN HOWARD

Painted panel from the cover of Invasion of the Cat-People. DWM's Terror of the Autons comic strip.

Cybermen bad guys' was all I ever needed to say, and he knew exactly what to do to sum the stories up beautifully.

It was the same with his paintings for *DWM* – "I want a really nice Sea Devil" or "We're doing a Robert Holmes special so I'm thinking something with Autons" and he'd come back with a marvellous trio of an Auton, a Drashig, and a Sontaran. Colin's flair for composition was brilliant. He really understood the need of a magazine cover as a sales point. The left-hand side, where the logo is, would always be seen more because of the way newsagents would display magazines in those days, meaning his use of rich colours and imagery always started on the left and drew the eye across right, making people want to pick the magazine up in a shop and see what the rest of the art was. An editors' dream, frankly. Go look at that Sea Devil cover for *DWM* 192 (my favourite of all the art Colin did for me at Marvel UK) or the fabulous Dalek cover he did for the 1993 *DWM* Summer Special. That's craftsmanship, that is.

In 1994, I was also starting to write books and did my first Missing Adventure for Virgin. They asked me who I wanted to paint the cover and I immediately said Colin. He was already being used extensively by BBC Video at this point, so asking him to squeeze a book cover into his schedule was tricky.

"What's it got to show?" he asked me.

"Cats in shiny leather spacesuits, on two feet, carrying BFGs. Oh, and I want my two cats Scratch and Tarot to act as your models." So, not much then. Colin also added his own lovely black-and-white cat Albert into the mix and I could not have been happier with the cover. It was exactly what I wanted. And, just to make it more complicated, the standard at the time was to paint the Doctor and companion in the sidebar – but I asked for both Ben and Polly alongside the Second Doctor. And rather than whine (well, not to me anyway), Colin made it work. I'm very proud to say that the original painting is framed and hangs on my wall in my home.

And now look where he is. Involved with animating old '60s black-and-white missing *Doctor Who* stories, his background paintings for *The Macra Terror* are amongst the very best the animation series has seen. Nearly thirty-five years on, and Colin is still heavily involved in this wacky, insane world of *Doctor Who* and so he should be. And now he has this book as a testament and a permanent record of all that he has achieved so far. He deserves it, and so do we fans.

LEE BINDING
Graphic Designer and Cover Artist.

I don't know if you know this, but there's almost a family tree of *Doctor Who* artists. I'm kind of down on the far left with the weird cousins, and near the top is lovely Colin Howard, which he'll hate me saying because Colin is genuinely modest about his considerable talent. Anyway, in that unintentional position, Colin has forged ahead and made oh-so-wonderful artwork that has set the benchmark for all of us to reference, to look up to, and definitely be motivated by. For me, Colin's got the most gorgeous ability to fill the canvas with faces and shapes and colour and wonder, and it looks totally composed and dynamic. It's a lot harder than it looks and yet Colin does this in every piece! We can only stare in wonderment.

Colin with Lee Binding.

One of the lovely things about fandom artists, particularly in *Who* fandom, is we all inspire and will inspire each other. That family tree of artists keeps on going, interacting, spreading. There's more of us than there ever was! And we all talk and share ideas, and look at each other's pieces and comment and share and ideas fizz between us. And this is no small thanks to people like Colin, who took the lead and gave us something to be creative with. Go look at these wonderful pictures here and feel your brain crackle with excitement. I hope you're as inspired by them as I am.

MARGARET HOPE
BBC Children's Books Design Manager, 1992-1999.

It feels like it was another dimension, another galaxy, when I joined BBC Worldwide as Children's books design manager back in 1992. At that time, there were three of us in the Children's dept. Rona Selby was the publisher, Nuala Buffini the editor, and me on design. From very small beginnings and limited resources, we created a stunning list of children's books, audio, and video/DVDs, which included many staple favourites: *Telebubbies, Pingu, Wallace & Gromit*, to name just three – and, of course, *Doctor Who*.

Like all children of the '60s, I grew up hiding behind the couch when Jon Pertwee fought the Master. It was the highlight of the week, along with *Top of the Pops*. Little did I know that, decades later, I would be filing through the BBC *Doctor Who* archive looking for images to use on fiction covers and the colour non-fiction books.

TIMESLIDES: THE DOCTOR WHO ART OF COLIN HOWARD

The *Doctor Who* series was off-air at that time, having slipped into a time warp in 1989. I recall the incredible fan base hounding the Beeb to bring back the Doctor. There was a TV film starring Paul McGann. This was an attempt to revive the series, made in partnership with Universal Studios and, as a result, it was light years away from the Doctor we loved, who is essentially very quirky, very British.

It would be many years before the Doctor reappeared on our screens, so it was our duty to keep the Doctor's story alive in print. We published one to two fiction titles a month, *The Seven Doctors'* series, and *The Eighth Doctor*. There were also big non-fiction colour titles like the *Doctor Who A-Z* and *Book of Monsters*. I spent many an hour poring over the amazing BBC archive of photos taken on set and behind the scenes.

As design manager, my job was to look after all the creative aspects of the books, marketing materials, audio/video sleeves… I would brief and art direct cover content and composition, ensuring continuity across the series. It was important to design a look that worked across all publishing for maximum impact and to satisfy the collectors. Yes, I too would line up all the spines to ensure they matched. We created a new logo for the aptly titled Regeneration of the *Doctor Who* publishing line. The wonderfully talented editor/author Steve Cole also joined us as editor on *Doctor Who* and we expanded rapidly. The adult department were keen to take over *Doctor Who*, as the genre was so reliable in creating revenue. The incredible fan base kept the Doctor alive, in purchasing every edition we published, and we all held fast.

So where did Colin feature in the process? Once I had all the information I needed i.e. the title, synopsis/draft manuscript and which Doctor, I would compile a brief for the artist. Colin was my go-to artist, my wing man. He was very knowledgeable on *Doctor Who* and a fantastic sci-fi illustrator. No brief was too challenging for him and he was super-fast, but most of all a total pleasure to work with. We had to work to some crazy deadlines, and it was important to maintain good working relationships with artists and external designers. I relied so heavily on their expertise and creative genius. Colin was never phased and could tackle any brief with creative flair. I also worked closely with a design group called Black Sheep.

Once artwork was complete, I would then co-ordinate all the different elements working to a schedule, to create the finished file for print. I liaised with other departments i.e. publicity, marketing, sales, and magazines to supply visual material in good time.

My time at the BBC was immensely enjoyable and I now look back and consider just how many gifted and talented people I worked with; Colin high amongst them. When I left in 1999, Colin created an awesome portrait of me as a Borg. The caption read "British Borg-casting Corporation. You will be assimilated! Lots of Love and good luck, Colin Howard".

It's one of my most treasured images and sums up Colin's creative genius and wit.

Like *Doctor Who*, Colin is and always will be an eternal legend.

JAMIE LENMAN
Artist, *Doctor Who Magazine*.

Too young for vinyl, too old for streams – kids of the '90s were the video generation. Saving up all my pocket money and blamming it in WHSmith was how I navigated my cultural landscape – from movie blockbusters to rock concerts and of course, *Doctor Who*.

With the series off air, those tapes were all we had, served up in random order without the week's wait between episodes. Looking back, there was no real need for anything more than a logo and a publicity photo on the boxes – we would have bought them regardless. But somebody, somewhere, decided that these things had to be beautiful, and boy were they. On shelves lit up like rainbows, in amidst a throng of gifted artists, you could always tell one of Colin's covers from the dazzling colours and jam-packed compositions. Each one was an explosion of detail, managing to make even *Time-Flight* look like an unmissable thrill ride. They almost felt restrained by the dimensions of the plastic packs, as if they were meant to be huge posters hanging off the walls, and I still wish BBC Worldwide had cottoned on and printed a few in this format.

When the videos moved beyond paintings and then everyone moved beyond videos, Colin's efforts stayed with me so much that when I was faced with a particularly challenging cover-commission of my own, I plucked up the courage to seek him out over the Internet and ask his advice. To my amazement, he not only replied with a lengthy reel of tips and tricks, he'd even taken the time to spruce up my rather pathetic original in areas where it was exceptionally lacking – all for a complete stranger who was essentially trying to rip off his stuff.

Years later, when I'd found my own style and was busy lending it to the pages of *Doctor Who Magazine*, I was lucky enough to be sat next to the man himself in the artists' room at a special convention. Happily, he proved to be every bit as generous and amiable in person as he was via email, one half of a great team with his wonderful wife Michelle. Since then we have remained firm friends, and he even turned up to a show on my album tour, wherein I duly puzzled the crowd by pointing him out and gibbering about *Red Dwarf Smegazine* (of which I have every copy that Colin's art graced).

Colin's work continues to inspire and astound me, from the private commissions he meticulously constructs to his deft and essential contributions to the animated reconstructions. I still have all those old tapes – the idea of jettisoning those beautiful covers is unthinkable – but at long last, this book will mean I don't have to leaf through that fabulous portfolio one cassette-case at a time.

NICK ABADZIS
Writer, Titan Comics' *The Tenth Doctor*, DWM's *The Betrothal of Sontar*.

Colin Howard is one of those *Doctor Who* artists who took the template created by Chris Achilléos and ran with it. Prior to Achilléos, *Doctor Who* illustration, which had existed mostly in Christmas annuals, *TV Comic*, ad campaigns, and upon the boxes of various toys, had been very much in the mould of a kind of genteel post-war children's illustration – thick inked lines, bright colours, reassuring avuncular figures admonishing drawings of men in monster suits, that sort of thing. There was something a bit Alfred E Bestall about it all (not a criticism, but he did lend a kind of heart-warming analeptic quality). With his Target book covers, Achilléos elevated *Who* illustration to the level of film poster advertising, even though his covers appeared on small paperback books that you'd buy with your pocket money.

Of all the artists that followed this breakthrough, Colin Howard is the one who really took it to the next level. The difference is that, unlike many of his predecessors in the Target range, who, after Achilléos, relied on certain aspects of comic book language for visual impact, Howard's illustrations used composition and light and shade as its main tools, for maximum dramatic effect.

You always recognised his work – his illustrations were always exquisite renderings, paintings that gave his subjects such form, depth and substance they almost sprang from the cover. Yes, in some cases they may have used familiar PR images as their source, but a Howard image was a portal into a vivid dimension where everything happened in 3D widescreen; they invited you to engage your visual imagination in a different way. Any Howard image immediately expanded the universe of *Doctor Who* and treated it with an exciting blockbuster sensibility. That a lot of his later work adorned the VHS line was an irony of sorts; his covers always promised the *Doctor Who* you remembered in your child's imagination and hid any budget limitations your adult's imagination might find more challenging to

TIMESLIDES: THE DOCTOR WHO ART OF COLIN HOWARD

gloss over. I think it's a big reason why the VHS line became such cherished objects of collectability – because they featured such great, enticing covers.

Colin Howard is a vital link in the evolution of *Doctor Who* art, from its pulpy origins to a thriving, sophisticated realm of print and industry in its own right. You wouldn't have got those artfully constructed DVD or later book covers without him proving that the true power of an image lies in beautifully considered construction.

MARTIN GERAGHTY
DWM Comic Artist; Character Artist, The Power of the Daleks, The Macra Terror, et al.

Doctor Who has always had the ability to attract top-drawer creative talent from the commercial art world, from Frank Bellamy's brilliant *Radio Times* illustrations in the '70s, through the range of incredible artists who have crafted a whole host of book covers, promotional cards, calendars, and comic strips right up to this day. All have added breadth and solidity to the good Doctor's adventures, extending the boundaries of the limited resources the programme-makers regularly contended with when bringing the show to our screens.

It was during the so-called Wilderness Years of the '90s when the TV show was off the air that I imagine most of us became aware of Colin's work, when it graced the covers of the monthly VHS releases, where his character likenesses, vibrant use of colour, and striking compositions could be spotted at twenty paces across a busy shop-floor.

As a great admirer of Colin's work over those years, it was a particular delight to work with him recently on the range of animated recreations of lost stories for the BBC Blu-ray range, his unique style being employed to add texture, rich colour, and detail to the locations of Cambridge in *Shada*, the future colony environs in *The Macra Terror*, and Maxtible's Canterbury residence in *The Evil of the Daleks*.

As a contributor to these productions myself, it was a joy to have access to the files which were updated daily – by a staggeringly small team of artists – with storyboards, new snippets of animation, and expansive vistas, both earthbound and alien. Colin's brief covered set-dresser and designer, stylist, prop-buyer, and scenic painter, and his lovingly rendered prop paintings (many incorporating blink-and-you'll-miss-them Easter eggs from the show's rich history), furniture, wallpapers, and backgrounds add weight, verisimilitude, and huge value to these productions.

After thirty-odd years of association with the show, and in an uncertain world, it's very gratifying to know he's still producing new artwork, both commercially and by private commission, that delights and enriches the *Doctor Who* universe and will continue to inspire young and old alike.

NEIL COLE
Curator, The Museum of Classic Sci-Fi.

Within our *Doctor Who*-centred genre kingdom, we live in an age where almost weekly a 'new artistic genius' is announced on social media. In 1915, an artistic protest group The Dadaists used a revolutionary new idea, 'photomontage' – the cutting up and pasting of photographs – to create fresh artworks with subversive meanings. Time-travel in your personal TARDIS a full century, and a raft of creative *Who*-fans have re-discovered the technique on their laptops and tablets, aided and abetted with powerful digital tools that allow for glorious blending, colouring, and 'glows'. Enter the current world of *Doctor Who* artwork (and, for that matter, cinema poster artwork) – the digital photomontage – recognisable photos (you've generally seen them before) arranged nicely, blended slickly onto a CGI background. I do these myself for a little fanzine I produce for my museum. They are comparatively quick and look pretty good. Readers are satisfied.

But 'artistic genius'? For me, the plaudits attached to this new body of artwork are slightly exaggerated. Please don't read me wrong – these digital composites absolutely require a solid aesthetic sensibility and a dedication to understanding and deploying software. But in all truth, for myself, you need to step into your TARDIS again and travel backward some thirty or forty years to meet serious, dedicated artistic talent. Switch off your laptop, lightbox, and screen. There is no 'undo' button where we are headed; just tubes of pure coloured pigment, a range of differently sized and shaped brushes, and plain, unblemished art paper.

I come to write this piece as someone who still draws and paints by hand and reluctantly creates digitally when necessary. The greatest artistic challenge for me remains the rendering of something unique and accurately on what begins as a blank page, with tubes of viscous liquid colours. If I think

Colin with Neil Cole, about to be menaced by a Terileptil.

hard about that description, it quite literally intimidates me. In my early twenties, I was studying physics and drawing occasional covers for small *Doctor Who* fanzines. At that time, there existed an elite group of artists who inspired me to push the boundaries of my art and what was possible with tubes of paint and a brush. One of these legendary artists is finally presented here in this glorious, overdue book.

I first became acquainted with Colin Howard's artwork with his cover work for *DWM*. It stood out from its peers by deviating away from the traditional, purely photographic reference material; it expanded upon its subject. That is, Colin allowed his imagination to steer his compositions, rather than have the necessary portrait head shots dominate the creative process.

Clearly, Colin is a commercial artist: his truly sublime run of *Doctor Who* VHS covers had a job to do – to represent each televised story and show off their leading cast members. But unlike his peers, Colin went the extra mile, adding unseen details and pushing his compositions to the limit. Furthermore, as the BBC VHS range progressed, each new cover seemed to see Colin continuing to push his artistic muscle. The compositions became ever more daring, his technique increasingly startling in its textural qualities and depth. I loved how Colin clearly espoused the use of a lightbox; unlike some artists, Colin would draw his likenesses free-hand and work on unique figurative poses resulting in completely distinctive cover work that was a galaxy away from the "copied from that photo" artworks many practitioners published.

So, to return to how I started this piece: artistic genius. In an age where a digital composite can be put together in a day or two by pulling together photographic images instantly from an almost infinite and instant wealth of online resources… stop for a moment. Imagine that blank sheet of paper. Imagine having to physically draw a truly realistic likeness by painstakingly working from observation, conjuring

TIMESLIDES: THE DOCTOR WHO ART OF COLIN HOWARD

up any visual element required of you – spacecraft, alien worlds and landscapes – from your imagination. And no 'undo' button. Artistic genius?

Just before lockdown, I had the incredible honour of having Colin and his lovely wife Michelle visit my small *Doctor Who* history museum in Northumberland. Talking to such a modest gentleman and artist who helped shape my own approach to my artwork was a privilege that I will treasure always. I'm very proud to have an original Howard hanging in the museum for fellow enthusiasts to see and appreciate.

ALEX SKERRATT
Screenwriter, *The Sooty Show.*

Doctor Who VHS covers were pretty instrumental in my becoming a *Doctor Who* fan. When I was nine, I was curious about getting into the show, but had no idea where to start – save for a line of intriguing volumes glistening on the shelves of HMV. They say you should never judge a book by its cover, but let's face it, we all do. And these were videos, anyway, so do the same rules apply?

Plus, deciding which *Doctor Who* video to buy was such a lottery, and when you were a newbie like me, you had very little information to go on apart from the sleeve blurb, and the cover artwork. (The cover for *Frontier in Space* is particularly clear in my mind – it looked like a movie poster!)

And like any good artwork, there was a certain joy in simply staring at it and appreciating it. I can remember as a child being driven back from my local HMV by my mum, ogling the artwork of the latest purchase, and being anxious to fire up the video player. Even when the tape was rolling, there was a thrill in being able to glance back at the sleeve, and then, of course, to see the new addition taking pride of place on the video shelf in the midst of the slowly growing collection… even if the spines didn't quite match up.

Of course, most of these were replaced with DVDs in the ensuing years, but I couldn't quite bring myself to throw out the videos. I clung to them, as if clinging to a part of my childhood, until about 2016. But even then, there were some tapes that were just too special, and even then, I couldn't allow those gorgeous video sleeves to go to landfill.

I removed them, one by one, and kept them all. And I always will.

PAUL SIMPSON
Editor, *Sci-Fi Bulletin.*

Much as I love artists who produce photo-realistic versions of characters and situations from TV series and films, reproducing poses that I've become very familiar with – and indeed have commissioned quite a few at various points during my editorial career – I have always had a soft spot for those who buy into the mythology around the subject they're treating. (I'm the same with novels: expand the universes with something that we'd never get to see on TV or the big screen!)

I still remember seeing Colin Howard's artwork for the first time in Peter Haining's *The Key to Time*, which, I think it's fair to say, had a wide variety of styles, not all of which were to my taste. His piece featuring the Silurians stood out because it did something different than portray a scene from the 1970 story, instead – just as Mac Hulke did in his novel based on the serial – fleshing out the race and giving them a life they didn't necessarily have on screen.

In the years that have followed, I've perhaps inadvertently collected Colin's work – not necessarily as prints, but on the covers of the many hundreds of pounds' worth of *Doctor Who* merchandise that I've purchased. While he may not always have the photographic feel of some of his contemporaries on the various ranges, you could always be sure of a sense of style and of environment – look at the *Warriors of the Deep* VHS cover for an example of this with its use of a portrait of Peter Davison in a different mode from the way he's usually depicted.

Of course, in recent times, Colin's work has also graced the animations that have brought back to life the lost TV episodes from the 1960s, and I'm hoping that we're in a temporary hiatus on those – just think what he could do with the marketplace in *The Crusades* or the wild coves in *The Smugglers*…

LEE SULLIVAN
Artist, Doctor Who Magazine, Candy Jar Books.

"It was the best of times, it was the worst of times…"

Charles Dickens' great opening line for *A Tale of Two Cities* has been borrowed many times, not least for that other great sci-fi franchise, *Star Trek*. But it applies precisely to that very particular time in *Doctor Who*'s history when it finally succumbed in 1989 to powers that dwarfed even those of the Daleks and Cybermen.

At the same time, a bunch of us would-be contributors who had grown up as fans from childhood were starting their careers as actors, writers, editors, publishers, model-makers, sculptors, and artists of various disciplines, all hoping to contribute to the show itself or its peripheral media. This was clearly the worst of times for all of them, wasn't it?

Well, as it turned out, it was actually the beginning of the best of times for some. As the show itself was gone, with no guarantee of a return to our screens either sooner or later, the hungry gaze of the Doctor's dedicated followers started to turn to the alternatives on view. Which, of course, brings us to the artist celebrated by this collection of work: the dear, talented creator of superlatively-painted cover artworks and all-round lovely man, Colin Howard.

Along with the burgeoning *New Adventures* series of novels from Virgin Books and the comic strips in *DWM*, the BBC video releases suddenly became even more significant than they had been, as fans started to trawl through the back-catalogue. The programmes were, of course, the main event, but – as with LP covers before the age of CDs – the covers themselves became part of the enjoyment of the videos too. Lingering over the artworks back then yielded a lot of pleasure for the owners and seeing them once more gives a pleasurable blast of nostalgia now.

I've seen this with my own eyes, as fans leaf through examples of Colin's work, each one bringing back so many memories. Sometimes, there is a certain amount of professional jealousy for other practitioners in one's chosen field. It's nothing to be proud of, but perhaps inevitable, given the insecurity of creative types. Not so with Colin's work. He may have the kind of talent and finishing techniques which would normally bring on a terrible, envious gnashing of my teeth, and of course, he's married to the even more lovely Michelle, but Colin is just too nice a human being for this to occur.

Enjoy these fine works and try – as I do – not to feel dizzy when you consider how much work has gone into creating them with such tiny, tiny brushes!

Colin with Lee.

TIMESLIDES: THE DOCTOR WHO ART OF COLIN HOWARD

PETE MCTIGHE
Screenwriter, *Kerblam!* and *Praxeus*; Booklet Notes, *Doctor Who: The Collection*.

Hello Colin Howard. We've never met, but you and your artwork are inextricably woven through my life and love of *Doctor Who*.

Those precious VHS releases that were issued in the 1990s were my first opportunity to obtain (alleged!) pristine copies of classic adventures I'd either seen just the once, or often never experienced at all. And the gorgeous cover illustrations were a huge part of the attraction and their collectability. Even now, when I think of *The Five Doctors*, I see your blazing orange montage in my mind's eye; I see your pulpy comic book interpretation of *Paradise Towers*, the intensity and rage of your *Inferno*, your gorgeous elevation of *The King's Demons*, and the beautifully sympathetic six-volume *Key To Time* season. Oh, I could eat the lot!

As an artist, you made your mark on a significant strand of *Doctor Who* merchandise that got us through those dreaded wilderness years. Your artwork still adorns my office shelves, whether wrapped around favourite VHS tapes, or punching out of those lively *Doctor Who Magazine* or *Classic Comics* covers.

And what a treat to now have your work collected into one volume. The book will sit proudly on my shelf – my non-fiction book collection is extensive but curated; only the best make it! And I'm proud to add yours in pride of place, so I can pour over those magnificent covers and relive the best of times…

Matthew Doe
Specialist in Production Used *Doctor Who* Artefacts and Props.

In terms of *Doctor Who* artists, I would say Colin sits alongside a very small handful of original professional artists who should each wear the t-shirt, "I am not *an* Artist. I am *the* Artist. One of the originals, you might say…"

Okay, so I've played with the words of that famous quote that we have all grown up to love and repeat in our own little weird and wonderful ways. But that's exactly what Colin is to me: one of the originals. For those who were lucky enough to be growing up with his wonderful art on the shelves of newsagents or in the video shops in form of VHS cover artwork, it was magical: you actually never knew what the artwork was going to be or who it was going to be by until it was released and on the shelf (yes, for those who have only grown up with the Internet, back then we actually had surprises that never got mass leaked before release).

The show can take you back to a place of happy times and amazing memories, and Colin's artwork does just the same. For me, it was his *Remembrance of the Daleks DWM* #167 front artwork; not only was it Colin's first *DWM* cover but it was also my favourite episode. I got floods of memories of watching that story for the first time on TV whenever I would pick up that magazine. I remember that we didn't get to re-watch that episode for another five years, when it finally made its way to VHS – I guess the artwork was our form of time travel.

Having worked with Colin on a project a few years ago – one of those "pinch me" moments, may I add! – I had the opportunity of obtaining the original artwork of *DWM* #167 direct from Colin, and it proudly sits in my office in all its glory. Now, I get to see the art fully in its raw form, with no reduction in size and no being covered up with elements of the magazine's informative text. Just have a look at any of the art in this book and see how much detail you can spot that you couldn't or didn't when it was released in its commercial form. I can assure you this will be not only fun but make you look at Colin's art in a whole different way.

TIMEWAVE

PHILIP BATES
Editor.

One of the best things in the world is wandering around a gallery with someone who means a lot to you. It's an incredible bonding experience, mulling over these immersive works together, being drawn into each piece, sharing what you love, your thoughts, inspirations, and memories.

That's what I wanted for *Timeslides*. I wanted to make sure the reader was guided through this stunning gallery of intricate, engaging, and much-loved pieces with a friend.

But let's rewind. One day, Shaun Russell, my boss at Candy Jar, rang me up and said, 'We're doing an artbook with Colin Howard.'

'That's fantastic,' I enthused. Still, it was a curious sales strategy; was Shaun going to phone up all potential buyers and flog his wares? "When's it out?" I asked. "Because I'm definitely buying that!"

"No, no," Shaun went on. "I want you to *edit* it."

I can't remember what I said exactly, but I'm sure it was a tumult of disbelief, a somersault of words, meanderings, and dribblings that ultimately meant "I'll do that in a heartbeat."

I grew up in the dark, denim-laden times known as the 1990s, so was only introduced to *Doctor Who* properly in 2005. We had DVDs and no real need for VHSes. So why did I pick up any videotapes I could find? Because of Colin's art, of course. A largely-redundant medium wasn't redundant if adorned with these paintings, which immediately grabbed you and refused to let go. To get the chance to work alongside Colin, to learn more about his wonderful work, to even chat with him one-to-one? That was a no-brainer.

I had the pleasure of talking to him about everything in this book and more. Emails. WhatsApp. Skype. It soon became clear that Colin is an amazing guy. Talented, yes, but also very thoughtful, witty, and determined. Not just someone whose art I admired. A heck of a nice bloke.

He sends me old sketches he stumbles upon and shows me the process of turning his illustrations into full-blown paintings. We both recommend TV shows. I send him photos of my dogs, Guinness and Lottie. In return, he sends me pictures of his gorgeous kittens. One morning, when I was interviewing him for this book, I received a parcel actually from Col; it included an art print of Karen Gillan in *Jumanji* that I'd asked him for, plus some special extra prints he'd added in, just because. Specifically, just because that's the sort of guy he is. And we'd chat about our shared love of The Killers after seeing them on the *Imploding the Mirage* tour. Those concerts, delayed by Covid, were a long time coming – the same can be said of a book about Colin's astounding contributions to that great unfolding text called *Doctor Who*.

I hope this book demonstrates who Colin is. If so, I'll have done my job. Because I wanted to make sure you were guided through this gallery with a friend. I know I was.

So, Col: here you go, mate. I hope you're as proud of *Timeslides* as I am.

(above) The TARDIS as featured on the cover of The Discontinuity Guide, *Virgin Publishing.*

TIMESLIDES: THE DOCTOR WHO ART OF COLIN HOWARD

WITH THANKS TO:

John Freeman, for giving me the chance to fulfil my childhood ambitions at *Doctor Who Magazine*, for helping me develop as an artist, for your warmth and sage-like advice in troubled times.

Colin Baker, 'Ol Sixie', you lovely man, for appreciating my art and being so kind as to write a testimonial of my abilities, both here and way back in timey-wimey.

Gary Russell for taking up the baton at *DWM* and *Classic Comics*, continuing to commission me, even at Virgin Publishing. Plus, of course, our shared love of Felis Catus, and the *Missing Adventure* that brought.

Margaret Hope (née Clarke) my Borg Queen, for helping me realise my dreams as an 'official' *Doctor Who* artist across video and book releases at the BBC. Thank you for your warmth, friendship, advice, and conciliatory lunches.

Charles Norton, for remembering me from a *DWM* interview and asking if I'd consider a return to *Doctor Who* with the animations.

Paul Vazquez, for being the very best best man and friend, since we first met at the Norwich DWAS local group in the '80s. Thank you for your kindness and generosity, and for sticking by me through my diagnosis when others fell aside.

Eamonn McGrath, another great friend from the Norwich DWAS local group, for all the laughs/rock/drinks company, and digital art assistance – and for somewhere to stay when I left home to work at HMV Norwich.

Shaun Russell at Candy Jar; without his and Andy Frankham-Allen's enthusiasm for *Doctor Who* art, this book wouldn't exist.

Philip Bates, for enduring hours of my drivel and turning it into comprehensive earthling dialect that's now going to burrow into your memory banks like one of Khan's Ceti Eels!

And most importantly for this book:

Christos Achilléos, without whose art, I would never have pursued this career avenue.

I'm so grateful to have had the chance to meet you and Tasha, and so happy you were as genuine, appreciative, and lovely as you were. Rest in Peace, you incredible man x

And of course, to all *Doctor Who* VHS cover art fans, who remember the amazing individual covers and the artists that created them in the 1990s, a far more varied and individual time, when each release was as eagerly awaited and anticipated as the novelisations.

Thank you all,